TAITTIRĪ

With the Commentary of
ŚAṄKARĀCĀRYA

Translated by
Swami Gambhirananda

Advaita Ashrama
(Publication House of Ramakrishna Math)
5 Dehi Entally Road • Kolkata 700 014

Published by
Swami Shuddhidananda
Adhyaksha, Advaita Ashrama
Mayavati, Champawat, Uttarakhand, India
from its Publication House, Kolkata
Email: mail@advaitaashrama.org
Website: www.advaitaashrama.org

First Edition, 1980
Tenth Reprint, November 2022
1M1C

ISBN 978-81-7505-024-2

Printed in India at
A. G. Printers
Kolkata 700 009

PREFACE TO THE SECOND EDITION

This edition of the *Taittirīya Upaniṣad* has been thoroughly revised by the author himself. In the matter of printing, in order to help the reader, more space is given between the translation of the text and the translation of the *bhāṣya*. In the references, where only the figures without the name of any book occur, they refer to passages in this particular Upaniṣad.

In the PREFACE to the previous edition of this Upaniṣad, it was mentioned as the 'eighth and the last to be published in the current series'. However, this is not 'the last', as one more important Upaniṣad, the *Chāndogya Upaniṣad*, has been translated by the author, and published by us in 1983, making it the ninth in this series.

7 September 1985 PUBLISHER
Janmāṣṭamī
Advaita Ashrama
Mayavati, Himalayas

PREFACE TO THE FIRST EDITION

The *Taittirīya Upaniṣad* is the eighth and the last to be published in the current series, each Upaniṣad being separately issued in its entirety in book form, from the author's highly appreciated and avidly read *Eight Upaniṣads*, published by us in two volumes.

In the translation of the commentary, the words quoted from the text by Śaṅkarācārya are given in italics. These are followed by commas and the English equivalents. Informative explanatory foot-notes have been added wherever necessary.

The *Taittirīya Upaniṣad* belongs to the *Yajur-Veda*. This Veda has been handed down to us, generation after generation, in two recensions: the Taittirīya and the Vājasaneyī. The Taittirīya recension is the older and more important of the two. It contains a Saṁhitā, a Brāhmaṇa, and an Āraṇyaka. The seventh, eighth, and ninth chapters of the *Taittirīya Āraṇyaka* constitute this Upaniṣad; and they are respectively known under the titles Śīkṣāvallī, Ānandavallī, and Bhṛguvallī. This Upaniṣad is very popular among those who learn Vedic chanting in the strictly traditional manner, followed by the *Mahānārāyaṇa Upaniṣad*, which is the concluding chapter of the *Taittirīya Āraṇyaka*.

Tradition has it that Ācārya Śaṅkara wrote his commentary first on this Upaniṣad. He defines the word '*upaniṣad*' in his introduction to this commentary as 'leading to acquisition of the knowledge of Brahman'. The first chapter, Śīkṣāvallī, concludes with an exhortation by the Vedic teacher to his students, on the eve of their returning home as *snātakas* after the completion of their studies, comparable to a Convocation Address of modern times, instructing them how to conduct themselves in the world. The second chapter, Ānandavallī, opens with a profound declaration: 'He who realizes Brahman attains the Supreme. . . .Brahman is truth, knowledge, and infinite.' This key statement reveals in a flash, with aphoristic brevity, the quintessence of the entire philosophy of the Upaniṣads. Further, it proclaims that this supreme Reality is the origin, ground, and goal of the world of experience, thus establishing the fundamental identity of this intimate world with the ultimate Reality. A gradation of higher and higher stages of happiness and bliss is presented towards the end of this chapter, taking a worthy human being—'a noble youth, in the prime of his age, most swift and alert, perfectly whole and resolute, most vigorous in health, laden with all riches, and of good learning'—as the basic unit in this calculus. The acme is reached in Brahman, the source of Bliss, beyond which there is nothing higher to aspire after. The third chapter, Bhṛguvallī, unfolds a touching scene, in which the son Bhṛgu approaches the father Varuṇa time and again in quest of truth and Knowledge. The father, with all the paternal care, love, and understanding, leads the son step by step through a thoroughgoing study of the human personality, which, according to this Upaniṣad, is made up of five sheaths (*kośas*)—the material, the vital, the psychical, the intellectual, and the intuitive—in the innermost core of which resides the Self of man, the Ātman, the source of all Bliss; nay, it is Bliss itself. The Bliss of Brahman-Ātman is perceivable on the perfection of desirelessness (*akāmahata*). It is enjoyed and experienced by one who realizes Brahman. That is the only real Bliss from which all this bliss that we experience in the world 'has separated like spray from the sea and with which it gets united again'. That is the uniqueness of this Upaniṣad. It shines in a class by itself.

It is our pleasure and privilege to offer this edition of the *Taittirīya Upaniṣad* to all seekers after Truth (*Satyam*) Knowledge (*Jñānam*) Infinity (*Anantam*), which is the nature and essence of the supreme Reality described so impressively in it.

1 September 1980
Mayavati

PUBLISHER

KEY TO TRANSLITERATION AND PRONUNCIATION

		Sounds like
अ	a	o in s*o*n
आ	ā	a in m*a*ster
इ	i	i in *i*f
ई	ī	ee in f*ee*l
उ	u	u in f*u*ll
ऊ	ū	oo in b*oo*t
ऋ	ṛ	somewhat between r and ri
ए	e	a in ev*a*de
ऐ	ai	y in m*y*
ओ	o	o in *o*ver
औ	au	ow in *now*
क	k	k
ख	kh	ckh in blo*ckh*ead
ग	g	g (hard)
घ	gh	gh in lo*g-h*ut
ङ	ṅ	ng
च	c	ch (not k)
छ	ch	chh in cat*ch h*im
ज	j	j
झ	jh	dgeh in he*dgeh*og
ञ	ñ	n (somewhat)
ट	ṭ	t
ठ	ṭh	th in an*t-h*ill

		Sounds like
ड	ḍ	d
ढ	ḍh	dh in go*dh*ood
ण	ṇ	n in u*n*der
त	t	French t
थ	th	th in *th*umb
द	d	th in *th*en
ध	dh	theh in brea*the h*ere
न	n	n
प	p	p
फ	ph	ph in loo*p-h*ole
ब	b	b
भ	bh	bh in a*bh*or
म	m	m
य	y	y
र	r	r
ल	l	l
व	v	in a*v*ert
श	ś	sh
ष	ṣ	sh in *sh*ow
स	s	s
ह	h	h
ं	ṁ	m in hu*m*
:	ḥ	half h in hu*h*!

LIST OF ABBREVIATIONS

Ā.G.	...	Ānanda Giri
Ai.	...	Aitareya Upaniṣad
Ai.Ā.	...	Aitareya Āraṇyaka
Āp.	...	Āpastamba Dharma-Sūtras
Bṛ.	...	Bṛhadāraṇyaka Upaniṣad
Ch.	...	Chāndogya Upaniṣad
Cit.	...	Cityupaniṣad
G.	...	Bhagavad Gītā
Gar.	...	Garuḍa Purāṇa
Gau.	...	Gautama Smṛti
Īś.	...	Īśā Upaniṣad
Ka.	...	Kaṭha Upaniṣad
Kau.	...	Kauṣītakī Upaniṣad
M.	...	Manu Saṁhitā
Mbh.	...	Mahābhārata
Mu.	...	Muṇḍaka Upaniṣad
Mud.	...	Mudgalopaniṣad
Pr.	...	Praśna Upaniṣad
Ś.	...	Śaṅkarānanda
Śv.	...	Śvetāśvatara Upaniṣad
Tai.Ā.	...	Taittirīya Āraṇyaka

TAITTIRĪYA UPANIṢAD

ॐ शं नो मित्रः शं वरुणः। शं नो भवत्वर्यमा। शं न इन्द्रो बृहस्पतिः। शं नो विष्णुरुरुक्रमः। नमो ब्रह्मणे। नमस्ते वायो। त्वमेव प्रत्यक्षं ब्रह्मासि। त्वामेव प्रत्यक्षं ब्रह्म वदिष्यामि। ऋतं वदिष्यामि। सत्यं वदिष्यामि। तन्मामवतु। तद्वक्तारमवतु। अवतु माम्। अवतु वक्तारम्।

ॐ शान्तिः शान्तिः शान्तिः ॥

ॐ सह नाववतु। सह नौ भुनक्तु। सह वीर्यं करवावहै। तेजस्वि नावधीतमस्तु मा विद्विषावहै।

ॐ शान्तिः शान्तिः शान्तिः ॥

(For translation etc. see I.i)

TAITTIRĪYA UPANIṢAD

PART I

On the Science of Pronunciation etc.

CHAPTER I

Salutation to That (Brahman) which is of the nature of consciousness, from which the whole universe was born, into which it gets dissolved, and by which it is sustained.

I bow down ever before those adorable Teachers by whom was explained all these Upaniṣads in the past, by taking into consideration the words, the sentences, and the means of valid knowledge.

With the grace of my Teacher, and for the benefit of those who prefer a clear exposition, I compose this explanation of this Upaniṣad that is the essence of (that section of the Vedas, called) the Taittirīya.

Introduction: In the preceding text[1] have been studied the obligatory duties that are meant for diminishing the accumulated sins, and the optional rites that are meant for people craving for results. Now is commenced the knowledge of Brahman with a view to eschewing the causes that lead to the performance of *karma*[2]. Desire must be the source of *karma*, since it stimulates action; for no impulsion to activity is possible in the case of those whose desires have been fulfilled, they

[1] The Taittirīya Āraṇyaka, of which this Upaniṣad forms a part.
[2] Rites, duties, etc. enjoined by scriptures.

being then established in their own Self as a result of the absence of desire. And fulfilment of desires follows from the desire for the Self[1] inasmuch as the Self, indeed, is Brahman, and for the knower of Brahman will be declared the attainment of the Highest (II. i. 1). Therefore the continuance in one's own Self, on the eradication of ignorance, is tantamount to the attainment of the Highest, which fact is supported by such Vedic texts as: '(When) one gets fearlessly established (in Brahman)' (II.vii.1), 'He attains this self made of bliss' (II.viii.5).

Objection: May it not be said that emancipation consists in remaining established in one's own Self without any positive effort—a state that ensues as a consequence of the non-commencement of optional and prohibited activities, the exhaustion through enjoyment of (the results of) *karmas* that have commenced, and the absence of sin owing to the performance of obligatory *karmas*. Or, (it may be that) emancipation results from the activities themselves, since *karmas* are the source of that unsurpassable happiness which is called heaven.

Answer: This cannot be so, because *karma* is multifarious, and as such, there is the possibility that there are actions—done in many previous births and bearing fruits (in this life) or remaining in abeyance—which have opposite results. Accordingly, since those of the actions that have not begun to bear fruits (in

[1] Really speaking, desire relates to the non-Self, and this ceases on the realization of the Self. Therefore 'the desire for the Self' is to be understood as implying an unfettered devotion to the Self with the idea that It alone is the Reality, and nothing else exists.

this life) cannot possibly become exhausted through enjoyment in (this) one single birth, it is reasonable that a fresh body shall be created as a result of the residual fruits of action; and the existence of residual fruits of work is also proved by hundreds of Vedic and Smṛti texts such as: 'Among them, those who were performers of meritorious deeds here, (they will attain good births)' (Ch. V. x. 7); 'Owing to the residual (results, the soul gets its future birth)' (Āp. II. 2.2.3; Gau. 11).

Objection: The obligatory duties are calculated to consume all the good and bad fruits of actions that are still inoperative.

Answer: No, for it is stated that the non-performance (of obligatory duties) entails *pratyavāya*. And the word *pratyavāya* means evil consequences. Since it is admitted that obligatory duties are meant for warding off evil consequence in the form of a future sorrow, they cannot be meant for consuming actions that have not begun to bear fruit. Granted, however, that the obligatory duties are capable of dissipating the actions that are yet inoperative, it is only the impure ones that they can sweep away and not the pure ones; for there is no contradiction (between the pure actions and obligatory duties) inasmuch as the actions that have desirable results are pure by nature, and, as such, they cannot be logically opposed to obligatory duties, the pure and the impure alone being reasonably opposed to each other.

Moreover, since desires, which are the springs of action, cannot cease unless there is enlightenment, there is no possibility of the eradication of actions as a whole (by the obligatory duties). And it has been said that since desire has for its objects things other than the Self, it belongs to one who has not realized the Self; that there can be no desire in one's own Self, It being ever realized;[1] and that the Self is the supreme Brahman. Besides, the non-performance of obligatory duties is a negation, from which an evil consequence cannot reasonably follow;[2] hence the non-observance of the obligatory duties is a pointer to the fruition of the evil consequences flowing from the sins accumulated in the past. Accordingly, the use of the suffix *śatṛ* (-ing) is not unreasonable in the text: 'Not performing the obligatory duty (and performing the prohibited ones and getting attached to sense-objects, a man courts his downfall)'[3] (M. XI.44). Else there will emerge a positive entity from a non-entity, which fact will nullify all means of valid knowledge. Therefore, it is not proved that a man, (as a result of *karma*,) remains

[1] 'To those who see everything as the Self, there can be really no object (of desire) and hence there is no possibility of desire'.—Ā.G.

[2] 'A future sorrow is called a *pratyavāya*, which being a positive entity, cannot have a non-entity as its cause. For according to the Vedic text, "Sin arises from sin" (Bṛ. IV. iv. 5), sorrow is caused by the performance of prohibited actions.'—Ā.G.

[3] The use of the *śatṛ* (-ing) along with a negative (in 'not performing') cannot be construed to mean that non-performance is the cause of downfall, since the sentence bears a more reasonable interpretation. For good people point to evil consequences thus: 'Had there been a proper performance of obligatory and occasional duties, there would have been an attenuation of accumulated sins. But this man did not perform the enjoined duties; hence there must be *pratyavāya* (i.e. non-elimination of future sorrow)'. Non-performance is thus only a pointer and not a cause.

poised in his Self without any positive (spiritual) effort.

As for the statement, 'emancipation is attainable through activity inasmuch as the unsurpassable happiness, called heaven, is a result of *karma*', that too is wrong. For emancipation is a permanent entity, and nothing that is everlasting can ever have a beginning. Whatever is produced in this world is impermanent. Therefore, emancipation is not a creation of *karma*.

Objection: *Karma* in association with meditation (and worship) has the capacity of producing a permanent thing.

Answer: No, because that involves a contradiction. It is self-contradictory to say that a thing that is eternal is still created.

Objection: Since the very thing which is destroyed cannot be produced again, therefore liberation, though permanent, can be brought into existence just like non-existence in the form of destruction (which is brought about by action).[1]

Answer: No, for freedom is a positive entity.[2] (Moreover) since non-existences, (as such), cannot be distinguished, it is a mere fancy to aver that non-existence

[1] According to the Nyāya philosophy, non-existences are of four kinds: (i) absolute non-existence (*atyantābhāva*), (ii) mutual non-existence (*anyonyābhāva*), (iii) non-existence in the form of destruction (*pradhvaṁsābhāva*), and (iv) previous non-existence (*prāgabhāva*). As regards the third kind of non-existence, it occurs where a thing, e.g. a pot, is broken. Since that very pot cannot be created over again, the destruction, once brought about continues for eternity. Or, in other words, the destruction is created, but it is eternal. Similarly, a created salvation can be eternal.

[2] And not a non-existence, which destruction is.

in the form of destruction has a beginning.[1] Non-existence is in fact that which is opposed to existence. On the analogy that existence, though one, is differentiated by a pot or a cloth, as the *existence* of a pot or the *existence* of a cloth, as though they are different, the non-existence of existence, too, though undifferentiated, is imagined to be differentiated—just as substances etc. are—owing to the (fancied) association (with them) of action, quality, etc. Not that a non-existence can coexist with a quality in the sense that a lotus does (with its colour etc.). Should it be possessed of an adjective, it will become nothing but existence.[2]

Objection: Since the agent of meditation and action is eternal, the salvation emerging as a result of a flow of meditation and action[3] is eternal.

Answer: No. For the agentship that flows like the current of the Gaṅgā is an evil in itself, and salvation

1 It is wrong to deny a beginning for other forms of non-existence while allowing it for destruction only. Nyāya believes that emancipation means destruction of sorrow and nothing positive.

2 An adjective co-exists with a noun. Now non-existence cannot co-exist with its counterpart—a positive attribute—though the latter is prefixed to it as an adjective (as in *ghaṭābhāva*—a pot's non-existence); for if co-existence were possible, then on the assumption that *pradhvaṁsābhāva* is eternal, its adjectival counterpart, viz pot, would also become eternal. Moreover, if it co-exists with the pot, then it cannot be non-existence, for existence and non-existence are mutually exclusive. Therefore, the supposition that different classes of non-existences can be distinguished is only an error arising from similar concepts pertaining to their positive counterparts.

3 Since the means flow as a constant current, the end, too, will go on flowing concurrently and eternally.

will be subject to cessation on the cessation of agentship.[1] Therefore, emancipation consists in continuance in one's own Self on the cessation of the material cause in the form of ignorance, desire, and activity. The Self, as such, is Brahman; and from the knowledge of Brahman follows liberation consisting in the eradication of ignorance. Hence is commenced (this) Upaniṣad meant for to lead to the acquisition of the knowledge of Brahman. Knowledge (itself) is referred to by the word Upaniṣad, for, in the case of those who are devoted to it, it either loosens or ends such things as being born in a womb and old age, or because it takes one near Brahman, or because the highest good is proximately embedded in it. And the book, too, is called an Upaniṣad because it is meant for that purpose.

शं नो मित्रः शं वरुणः । शं नो भवत्वर्यमा । शं न इन्द्रो बृहस्पतिः । शं नो विष्णुरुरुक्रमः । नमो ब्रह्मणे । नमस्ते वायो । त्वमेव प्रत्यक्षं ब्रह्मासि । त्वामेव प्रत्यक्षं ब्रह्म वदिष्यामि । ऋतं वदिष्यामि । सत्यं वदिष्यामि । तन्मामवतु । तद्वक्तारमवतु । अवतु माम् । अवतु वक्तारम् । ॐ शान्तिः शान्तिः शान्तिः ॥१॥ इति प्रथमोऽनुवाकः ॥

1. May Mitra be blissful to us. May Varuṇa be blissful to us. May Aryaman be blissful to us. May Indra and Bṛhaspati be blissful to us. May Viṣṇu, of

[1] If agentship flows on unceasingly, there will be no emancipation; and if the flow stops, emancipation too will stop.

long strides, be blissful to us. Salutation to Brahman. Salutation to you, O Vāyu. You, indeed, are the immediate Brahman. You alone I shall call the direct Brahman. I shall call you righteousness. I shall call you truth. May he protect me. May he protect the teacher. May he protect me. May he protect the teacher. *Om*, peace, peace, peace!

May Mitra, the deity who identifies himself with and is the self of the function of exhaling and of day; become *śam*, blissful; *naḥ*, to us. Similarly, too, Varuṇa is the deity who identifies himself with and is the self of the function of inhaling and of night. Aryaman identifies himself with the eye and the sun, Indra with strength, and Bṛhaspati with speech and intellect. Viṣṇu is *urukramaḥ*, possessed of great strides, and identifies himself with the feet. These are the deities in the context of the body. The expression, *śam naḥ bhavatu*, may he be blissful to us, is to be connected with all. Since the comprehension, retention, and communication of the knowledge of Brahman can proceed without hindrance when the gods are benevolent, their benignity is being prayed for by saying, *śam naḥ bhavatu* etc. Salutation and eulogy are offered to Vāyu (Air) by one craving for the knowledge of Brahman, so that the hindrances to the knowledge of Brahman may be averted. Since the fruits of all actions are in his keeping, Vāyu is Brahman; *brahmaṇe*, to that Brahman; *namaḥ*, (humble) salutation; the expression, 'I offer', has to be added to complete the sentence. *Namaḥ*, salutation; *te*, to you; *vāyo*, O Vāyu; i.e. I salute you. Thus Vāyu (Air, Life) himself is referred to both mediately and immediately. Besides, (O Air), since *tvam eva asi*, you yourself are; *pratyakṣam brahma*, the direct and immediate Brahman — being proximate and without any intervention, as contrasted with outer organs like the eye etc.; therefore, *vadiṣyāmi*, I shall call; *tvām eva*, you alone; as *pratyakṣam brahma*, the direct and immediate Brahman.[1] *Ṛtam*, righteousness, is an idea fully ascertained by the intellect in accordance with the scriptures and in conformity with practice; that, too, being subject to you, *vadiṣyāmi*, I shall speak of you alone as that (*ṛta*). *Satyam*, truth, is that which is reduced to practice through speech and bodily action; since that truth, too, is practised under you, *vadiṣyāmi*, I shall call you that truth. May *tat*, that, the all-pervasive Brahman, called Vāyu, being thus prayed to by me who hanker after knowledge; *avatu mām*, protect me — by endowing me with knowledge. May *tat*, that very Brahman; *avatu*, protect; *vaktāram*, the teacher — by endowing him with the power of exposition. The repetition of the expressions, *avatu mām avatu vaktāram*, is for showing eagerness (for knowledge). The three repetitions in *Om śāntiḥ*, *śāntiḥ*,

[1] Brahman is referred to indirectly by such words as, 'That', and directly by the word Vāyu; for Vāyu, in the form of the vital force (*prāṇa*) is directly perceived, though as *sūtra* (Hiraṇyagarbha linking up all) he is known indirectly. The life force is more directly cognized than the sense-organs like the eye etc., which have to be inferred from the fact of their perceiving colour etc. The vital force is directly cognized by the witness (Self); and as compared with the sense-organs, it is nearer to the Self. Besides, the word Brahman, derivatively means that which nourishes. The vital force nourishes the body; therefore, with regard to the body it is Brahman.

śāntiḥ, (*Om*, peace, peace, peace) are for destroying the three kinds of obstacles to the acquisition of knowledge, viz the physical, the natural, and the supernatural.

CHAPTER II

ॐ शीक्षां व्याख्यास्यामः। वर्णः स्वरः। मात्रा बलम्। साम सन्तानः। इत्युक्तः शीक्षाध्यायः॥१॥ इति द्वितीयोऽनुवाकः॥

1. *Om*! We shall speak of the science of pronunciation. (The things to be learnt are) the alphabet, accent, measure, emphasis, uniformity, juxtaposition. Thus has been spoken the chapter on pronunciation.

The chapter 'On the Science of Pronunciation' is begun so that there may not be any slackness in the effort involved in the recital of the text; for the comprehension of meaning plays a prominent part in the Upaniṣad.[1] *Śikṣā*, (derivatively) signifying that through which something is learnt, is the science of pronunciation of letters etc. Or, from the (derivative) implication of those things that are learnt, *śikṣā* means the letters etc. *Śīkṣā* is the same as *śikṣā*, the lengthening (of *i*) being a Vedic licence. That *śīkṣām*, science of

[1] Comprehension of meaning is dependent on proper pronunciation; and slackness in effort refers to errors in pronunciation.

pronunciation; *vyākhyāsyāmaḥ*, we shall explain — (derivatively meaning) we shall speak (*khyāsyāmaḥ*) clearly (*vi*) and fully (*ā*). This form of the verb, signifying as it does the revelation of the activity (of the organ of speech), is derived from the root *cakṣiṅ* which optionally changes into *khyā*, and is preceded by *vi* and *ā*. Now, the *varṇaḥ*, alphabet, consists of *a* etc. The *svaraḥ*, accent, is *udātta* (elevated) etc. (*svaritaḥ*, pitched; and *anudātta*, unaccented). The *mātrāḥ*, measures (the times required to pronounce), are short etc. *Balam*, emphasis, is the kind of effort (in pronunciation). *Sāmaḥ* is uniformity — the medium mode of pronunciation of letters. *Santānaḥ* is the same as *saṁhitā*, i.e. juxtaposition (conjoining of the letters etc.). This is, indeed, what is to be taught. This *śīkṣādhyāyaḥ*, chapter in which *śīkṣā* occurs; *uktaḥ*, has been spoken; *iti*, thus. The conclusion with the word *uktaḥ*, is for the sake of making the way clear for what follows.

CHAPTER III

सह नौ यशः । सह नौ ब्रह्मवर्चसम् ।
अथातः संहिताया उपनिषदं व्याख्यास्यामः ।
पञ्चस्वधिकरणेषु । अधिलोकमधिज्यौतिषमधिविद्यमधि-प्रजमध्यात्मम् । ता महासꣳहिता इत्याचक्षते । अथाधिलोकम् । पृथिवी पूर्वरूपम् । द्यौरुत्तररूपम् । आकाशः सन्धिः ॥१॥

1. May we both attain fame together. May spiritual preeminence be vouchsafed to both of us together.

Now, therefore, we shall state the meditation on juxtaposition through five categories—relating to the worlds, to the shining things, to knowledge, to progeny, and to the body. These they call the great juxtapositions. Now then, as regards the meditation on the worlds: The earth is the first letter. Heaven is the last letter. The sky is the meeting-place.

Now is being stated the (esoteric) meditation on the *saṁhitā* (conjoining of letters). There, again, may the *yaśaḥ*, fame—which is prayed for as a reward for the full knowledge of the (esoteric) meditation on the *saṁhitā* etc.; come. *saha*, simultaneously; *nau*, to us both—to the teacher and the taught. And the *brahmavarcasam*, spiritual preeminence, splendour, that results from it; may that, too, occur *saha*, simultaneously; *nau*, to us both. This is an expression of a prayer on the part of the pupil. For, in the case of a pupil a prayer is appropriate, since his aspiration still remains unrealized. But this is not a prayer of the teacher, as he has gained the goal. For a teacher is called so when his aspiration has been fulfilled.

Since the intellect that is too much occupied with (verbal) texts cannot easily be led to the domain of comprehension of meaning, *ataḥ*, therefore; *atha*, after this, after the codification of the science of study; *vyākhyāsyāmaḥ*, we shall state; *upaniṣadam saṁhitāyāḥ*, the Upaniṣad, i.e. meditation, with regard to the *saṁhitā* (conjoining of letters)—a subject that is closely related to the (verbal) text itself; *pañcasu adhikaraṇeṣu*, under five headings—through five means, i.e. subjects of knowledge. Which are they? They are being enumerated; *adhilokam*, the meditation that refers to the worlds; similarly, *adhijyautiṣam*, meditation concerning lights; *adhividyam*, meditation concerning knowledge; *adhiprajam*, meditation concerning progeny; *adhyātmam*, meditation concerning the body.[1] The people versed in the Vedas, *ācakṣate*, speak of; *tāḥ*, these—these meditations concerning five subjects—; as *mahāsaṁhitāḥ*, the great juxtapositions—they being great, since they relate to great things like the world, and being *saṁhitās* (juxtapositions) as well. *Atha*, now then; from among all these, as they are presented seriatim, *adhilokam*, the meditation with reference to the worlds, is being stated. The word *atha* is used everywhere to show the order (of meditation). *Pṛthivī*, the earth; is *pūrvarūpam*, the earlier form, the earlier letter; this amounts to saying that one should think of the first letter, occurring in a juxtaposition, as the earth. Similarly, the *uttararūpam*, the last letter; is *dyauḥ*, heaven. *Ākāśaḥ*, sky (or space); is *sandhiḥ*, the middle one, between the first and the last letters, since in it the first and last forms get united.

वायुः सन्धानम् । इत्यधिलोकम् । अथाधिज्यौतिषम् ।
अग्निः पूर्वरूपम् । आदित्य उत्तररूपम् । आपः सन्धिः ।
वैद्युतः सन्धानम् । इत्यधिज्यौतिषम् । अथाधिविद्यम् ।
आचार्यः पूर्वरूपम् ॥२॥

[1] As one thinks of an image as Viṣṇu, so one can think of the different factors in a juxtaposition as the deities that preside over them, the meditation being on the deities and not on the things that are enumerated under the five categories.

अन्तेवास्युत्तररूपम्। विद्या सन्धिः। प्रवचनꣳ सन्धानम्। इत्यधिविद्यम्। अथाधिप्रजम्। माता पूर्वरूपम्। पितोत्तर-रूपम्। प्रजा सन्धिः। प्रजननꣳ सन्धानम्। इत्यधिप्रजम् ॥३॥

अथाध्यात्मम्। अधरा हनुः पूर्वरूपम्। उत्तरा हनुरुत्तर-रूपम्। वाक्सन्धिः। जिह्वा सन्धानम्। इत्यध्यात्मम्। इतीमा महासꣳहिताः। य एवमेता महासꣳहिता व्याख्याता वेद। संधीयते प्रजया पशुभिः। ब्रह्मवर्चसेनान्नाद्येन सुवर्ग्येण लोकेन ॥४॥ इति तृतीयोऽनुवाकः ॥

2-4. Vāyu is the link. This is the meditation with regard to the worlds. Then follows the meditation with regard to the shining things. Fire is the first letter. The sun is the last letter. Water is the rallying point. Lightning is the link. This is the meditation with regard to the shining things. Then follows the meditation with regard to knowledge. The teacher is the first letter. The student is the last letter. Knowledge is the meeting-place. Instruction is the link. This is the meditation with regard to knowledge. Then follows the meditation with regard to progeny. The mother is the first letter. The father is the last letter. The progeny is the focal point. Generation is the link. This is the meditation with regard to progeny. Then follows the meditation with regard to the (individual) body. The lower jaw is the first letter. The upper jaw is the last letter. Speech is the meeting-place. The tongue is the link. This is the meditation with regard to the (individual) body. These are the great juxtapositions. Anyone who thus meditates on these great juxtapositions, as they are explained, becomes conjoined with progeny, animals, the splendour of holiness, edible food, and the heavenly world.

Vāyuḥ, air, is; *sandhānam*, the link (a catalytic agent) —derived in the sense of that by which things are conjoined.[1] *Iti*, thus far—is stated; *adhilokam*, the meditation with reference to the worlds. *Atha adhijyautiṣam* etc. are to be similarly explained. The two words, *iti* and *imāḥ*, thus and these, allude to what was mentioned earlier. *Yaḥ*, anyone who; *evam*, thus; *veda*, meditates; on *etāḥ mahāsaṁhitāḥ*, these great juxtapositions; *vyākhyātāḥ*, as explained—. The meaning of the word *veda* should be *upāsanā*, meditation or adoration, because the topic is of perfect knowledge,[2] and because there is the text: 'Thus, O Prācīnayogya, you worship' (I.vi.2). And meditation consists in a current of uniform concepts, not interspersed with dissimilar ones, which proceeds according to the scriptures and relates to an object enjoined in the scriptures. Besides, the word *upāsanā* is well known in the world in such sentences as, 'He *upāsate*, waits on (i.e. adores), the Guru',

[1] 'To illustrate: In the text *iśe tvā*, the *e* that follows the *ś* is the symbol of the earth; the *t* that follows is identical with heaven; the intermediate space between these two letters is *ākāśa* (the tryst); the other *t* that emerges by duplication in that space as a result of the process of conjoining the two parts—the actual pronunciation being *iśet-tvā*—is identified with Vāyu (the joining agent). This is how one should meditate.'—Ś.

[2] If this meditation is resorted to by one who desires rewards, he gets these only. But this again leads a desireless man to knowledge of Brahman, and the second objective is aimed at by this Upaniṣad.

'He *upāsate*, waits on (i.e. adores), the king'; for a man who constantly serves the Guru and others is said to be rendering *upāsanā* (adoration to them); and he acquires the fruit of his adoration. Similarly, in the present context, too, he who meditates thus, *sandhīyate*, is conjoined with the things beginning from progeny and ending with heaven; that is, he acquires the fruits such as progeny and others.

CHAPTER IV

यश्छन्दसामृषभो विश्वरूपः। छन्दोभ्योऽध्यमृतात्संबभूव। स मेन्द्रो मेधया स्पृणोतु। अमृतस्य देव धारणो भूयासम्। शरीरं मे विचर्षणम्। जिह्वा मे मधुमत्तमा। कर्णाभ्यां भूरि विश्रुवम्। ब्रह्मणः कोशोऽसि मेधया पिहितः। श्रुतं मे गोपाय। आवहन्ती वितन्वाना ॥१॥

कुर्वाणाऽचीरमात्मनः। वासाꣳसि मम गावश्च। अन्नपाने च सर्वदा। ततो मे श्रियमावह। लोमशां पशुभिः सह स्वाहा। आमायन्तु ब्रह्मचारिणः स्वाहा। विमाऽऽयन्तु ब्रह्मचारिणः स्वाहा। प्रमाऽऽयन्तु ब्रह्मचारिणः स्वाहा। दमायन्तु ब्रह्मचारिणः स्वाहा। शमायन्तु ब्रह्मचारिणः स्वाहा ॥२॥

1-2. The *Om* that is preeminent in the Vedas, that pervades all words, and that emerged from the immortal Vedas as their quintessence, may he who is Indra (i.e. *Om*) gratify me with intelligence. O Lord, may I be the receptacle of immortality. May my body be fit; may my tongue be surpassingly sweet; may I hear much through the ears. You are the sheath of Brahman; you are covered by (worldly) wisdom. Protect what I have heard. Then vouchsafe to me who am her (i.e. Prosperity's) own, that Prosperity which brings, increases, and accomplishes quickly for me clothes, cattle, food, and drink for ever, and which is associated with furry and other animals. *Svāhā*. May the Brahmacārins (i.e. students) come to me from all sides. *Svāhā*. May the Brahmacārins come to me in various ways. *Svāhā*. May the Brahmacārins come to me in the proper way. *Svāhā*. May the Brahmacārins have physical self-control. *Svāhā*. May the Brahmacārins have mental self-control. *Svāhā*.

In the text beginning with *yaḥ chandasām* are being mentioned, for him who wants intelligence and wealth, a prayer and a sacrifice which are the means for their acquisition; and this conclusion is borne out by the indications implied in, 'May he who is Indra gratify me with intelligence', and 'Then bring for me wealth'. *Yaḥ*, he who; *chandasām*, among the Vedas; is *ṛṣabhaḥ*, a bull—like a bull, because of preeminence; *viśvarūpaḥ*, omniform—because of permeating all speech, in accordance with another Vedic text, 'For instance, as (all leaves are held together) by their midribs, (in this way all the words are joined together by *Om*)' (Ch.II. xxiii.3)—. Hence is *Om* a bull. *Om* is indeed the object to be worshipped here; hence its eulogy through such words as 'bull' is quite appropriate. *Chandobhyaḥ*, from the Vedas; *amṛtāt*, from immortality—the Vedas are indeed, immortal—, from that immortality; *adhisambabhūva*, was born super-excellently. The idea is that, *Om* appeared as the quintessence when Prajāpati performed austerity (i.e. deliberated intently) with a view to extracting the finest essence from the worlds, the gods, the Vedas and the *Vyāhṛtis* (*Bhūḥ*, *Bhuvaḥ*, *Svaḥ*). (It was only a revelation to him), for in the case of *Om*, which is everlasting, no real origination can properly be imagined. *Saḥ*, he—the *Om* which is of this kind; and which is *indraḥ*, the ordainer of all desires, the supreme Lord; *spṛṇotu*, may (He) gratify or strengthen—for the strength of wisdom is the object prayed for; *mā*, me; *medhayā*, with wisdom. *Deva*, O God; *bhūyāsam*, may (I) become; *dhāraṇaḥ*, the wearer; *amṛtasya*, of immortality—of the knowledge of Brahman which is the cause of immortality, this being the context of that knowledge.[1] Moreover, may, *me*, my; *śarīram*, body; become *vicarṣaṇam*, skilful, i.e. fit. The verb *bhūyāsam* (in the first person) should (here) be changed into *bhūyāt* in the third person. (May) *me*, my; *jihvā*, tongue; (become) *madhumattamā*, exceedingly sweet, i.e. abundantly possessed of sweet speech. *Karṇābhyām*, through the ears; *viśruvam* (i.e. *vyaśravam*), may I hear, that is, may I become a hearer of; *bhūri*, much. The meaning of the passage is that the group of

[1] Unless a man has intelligence, he cannot acquire knowledge of Brahman. Hence even a prayer for intelligence is meant for that knowledge. And since a poor man cannot purify his heart by scriptural rites, he must perform a sacrifice which is calculated to make him wealthy. Thus such a sacrifice, too, is an indirect aid to knowledge.

my body and senses should become fit for the knowledge of the Self.

For the same purpose, intelligence, too, is being prayed for. *Brahmaṇaḥ*, of Brahman, of the supreme Self; *asi*, you are; the *kośaḥ*, sheath—like the scabbard of a sword, you being the seat of realization. Indeed, you are the symbol of Brahman, on you is Brahman realized. (You are) *pihitaḥ*, covered; *medhayā*, by worldly intelligence; i.e. you who are such, are not known in your reality by people of ordinary intellect. (You) *gopāya*, protect; *me śrutam*, things that have been heard by me, the knowledge etc. of the Self that I have acquired through hearing. The idea is: Vouchsafe it that there may be acquisition of it, and no forgetfulness etc. These *mantras* are meant to be used for self-repetition by one who wants intelligence.

Now are being stated the *mantras* to be used for offering oblations by one who wants prosperity.

Since prosperity to an unwise man is surely a cause of evil, therefore, *tataḥ*, after that, after vouchsafing intelligence; *āvaha*, bring; *śriyam*, the (Goddess of) Prosperity; who is *āvahantī*, a bringer; *vitanvānā*, an increaser—for the root *tan* implies   kind of action; (*sarvadā*, ever); *kurvāṇā*, an accomplisher; *acīram*, soon—*acīram* being the same as *aciram*, the lengthening (of *i*) is being a Vedic licence; or the reading may be, *ciram kurvāṇā*, an accomplisher for ever; *ātmanaḥ mama*, for myself who belong to Prosperity herself. (Bringer etc.) of what? That is being said: *vāsāṁsi*, clothes; *ca*, and; *gāvaḥ*, i.e. *gāḥ*, cattle; *ca annapāne*, and food and drink. (Bring) the Prosperity that, *sarvadā*, for ever, accomplishes all these. Prosperity of what kind? *Lomaśām*, furry — (Prosperity that is) endowed with goats, sheep etc.; (*saha*,) together with — (Prosperity that is) endowed with other *paśubhiḥ*, animals. From the context, as determined by '*āvaha*, bring', it follows that *Om* itself is to be connected (with *āvaha* as its nominative). The utterance of *svāhā* is for indicating the end of the *mantras* meant for offering an oblation. The construction of *ā* is with the remote word *yantu* thus: *āyantu mām* (*brahmacāriṇaḥ*), may the Brahmacārins come to me (from all sides). Similarly, may *brahmacāriṇaḥ*, the Brahmacārins; *vi mā āyantu*, come to me variously; *pra mā āyantu*, come to me in a proper way;[1] *damāyantu*, be controlled in body; *śamāyantu*, be controlled in mind, etc.

यशो जनेऽसानि स्वाहा। श्रेयान् वस्यसोऽसानि स्वाहा। तं त्वा भग प्रविशानि स्वाहा। स मा भग प्रविश स्वाहा। तस्मिन् सहस्रशाखे निभगाहं त्वयि मृजे स्वाहा। यथाऽऽपः प्रवता यन्ति यथा मासा अहर्जरम्। एवं मां ब्रह्मचारिणः। धातरायन्तु सर्वतः स्वाहा। प्रतिवेशोऽसि प्र मा भाहि प्र मा पद्यस्व ॥३॥ इति चतुर्थोऽनुवाकः ॥

3. May I become famous among people. *Svāhā*. May I become praiseworthy among the wealthy. *Svāhā*. O adorable One, may I enter into you, such as you are. *Svāhā*. O venerable One, you, such as you are, enter into me. *Svāhā*. O adorable One, who are greatly

[1] *Vimāyantu* and *pramāyantu* are also interpreted thus: 'May they be sincere towards me, may they be recipients of valid knowledge.'

diversified, may I purify my sins in you. *Svāhā.* As water flows down a slope, as months roll into a year, similarly O Lord, may the students come to me from all quarters. *Svāhā.* You are like a resting house; so you become revealed to me, you reach me through and through.

Asāni, may I become; *yaśaḥ*, i.e. *yaśasvī*, famous; *jane*, among a multitude of people. *Vasyasaḥ* is the same as *vasīyasaḥ*, and means, from the supremely affluent or from him that excels all the wealthy; *śreyān*, more praiseworthy; *asāni*, may I become; this is the construction. Moreover, *tam tvā*, into you, such as you are—as the sheath of Brahman; *bhaga*, O venerable One; *praviśāni*, may I enter, and after entering, may I become identified, your very Self; this is the idea. *Saḥ*, you, too, such as you are; *bhaga*, O adorable One; *praviśa*, enter; *mā*, into me; let there be nothing but identity between us. *Tasmin*, in you, such as you are; *sahasraśākhe*, who are greatly diversified; *aham*, I; *nimṛje*, purify my sinful acts. In the world, *yathā*, as; *āpaḥ*, water; *yanti*, goes (flows); *pravatā*, down a sloping place; and *yathā*, as; *māsāḥ*, months; (roll into) *aharjaram*, the year—the year is *aharjara* since it, by undergoing change day be day, wears out people, or since the days get worn out, i.e. included in it; as the months go to it, *evam*, similarly; *dhātaḥ*, O Ordainer of everything; let *brahmacāriṇaḥ*, the Brahmacārins; *mām āyantu*, come to me; *sarvataḥ*, from all quarters. *Prativeśaḥ* means a resting-place, a house at hand. Thus, to those who are devoted to you, *prativeśaḥ asi*, you are like a rest-house, a place where all sorrows resulting from sin can be removed. Therefore, towards *mā*, me; *prabhāhi*, you reveal yourself; and *prapadyasva*, reach me through and through — make me full of you, i.e. identified with you, like gold soaked in mercury. The prayer for prosperity dealt with in this context of knowledge is for the sake of wealth. Wealth is needed for rites; and rites are meant to diminish accumulated sins — on the exhaustion of these, indeed, knowledge becomes revealed. Supporting this view there is this Smṛti: 'Just as one sees oneself on the clean surface of a mirror, so knowledge arises for man on the exhaustion of sin' (Mbh. Śā. 204.8; Gar. I. 237.6).

CHAPTER V

भूर्भुवः सुवरिति वा एतास्तिस्रो व्याहृतयः। तासामु ह स्मैतां चतुर्थीम्। माहाचमस्यः प्रवेदयते। मह इति। तद्ब्रह्म। स आत्मा। अङ्गान्यन्या देवताः। भूरिति वा अयं लोकः। भुव इत्यन्तरिक्षम्। सुवरित्यसौ लोकः ॥१॥

मह इत्यादित्यः। आदित्येन वाव सर्वे लोका महीयन्ते। भूरिति वा अग्निः। भुव इति वायुः। सुवरित्यादित्यः। मह इति चन्द्रमाः। चन्द्रमसा वाव सर्वाणि ज्योतींषि महीयन्ते। भूरिति वा ऋचः। भुव इति सामानि। सुवरिति यजूंषि ॥२॥

1-2. *Bhūḥ*, *Bhuvaḥ*, *Suvaḥ* — these three indeed are the *Vyāhṛtis*. Of them Māhācamasya knew a fourth one—*Maha* by name. It is Brahman; it is the Self. The other gods are the limbs. *Bhūḥ* indeed is this world. *Bhuvaḥ* is the intermediate space. *Suvaḥ* is the other world. *Maha* is the sun; through the sun, indeed, do all the worlds flourish. *Bhūḥ* indeed is the fire. *Bhuvaḥ* is the air. *Suvaḥ* is the sun. *Maha* is the moon; through the moon, indeed, all the luminaries flourish. *Bhūḥ* indeed is the Ṛg-Veda. *Bhuvaḥ* is the Sāma-Veda. *Suvaḥ* is the Yajur-Veda.

The meditation with regard to conjoining has been stated. After that have been dealt with, in an orderly way, the *mantras* for one who desires intelligence and prosperity. They, too, are indirectly helpful to knowledge. Then is being commenced the internal meditation on Brahman as identified with the *Vyāhṛtis*,[1] which has for its result the attainment of sovereignty (I.vi.2). The text *bhūḥ bhuvaḥ suvaḥ iti* is for drawing attention to what was stated (earlier). The statement *etāḥ tisraḥ*, these three, is for calling up to memory the ones that have been enumerated; and *vai* (indeed) is used for refreshing the memory with regard to the things called up. Thus we are reminded of these three well-known *Vyāhṛtis*. *Tāsām*, of these; this is the fourth *Vyāhṛti* called *Maha*. *Māhācamasyaḥ*, the son of Mahācamasa, *pravedayate*, knows—i.e. knew, or visualized, because

[1] *Bhūḥ*, *bhuvaḥ*, *suvaḥ*, etc., which stand for the respective worlds, are technically called the *Vyāhṛtis*. 'These *Vyāhṛtis* had been accepted with faith (by the student). If Brahman is now taught by ignoring them, will not be comprehended by the student's intellect. Hence Brahman embodied in the *Vyāhṛtis* as Hiraṇyagarbha, is being presented for his inward meditation.'—Ā.G.

(the particles) *u*, *ha*, and *sma*, refer to what is past—; *tām etām caturthīm*, this fourth one. The mention of Māhācamasya is by way of alluding to the seer (*Ṛṣi*). And from the fact of his mention in the instruction here, it is to be understood that the remembrance of the seer, too, forms a part of the meditation. The *Vyāhṛti* that was seen (discovered) by Māhācamasya, *mahaḥ iti*, as *Maha*; *tat*, that; is *brahma*, Brahman; for Brahman is great (*mahat*), and the *Vyāhṛti*, too, is *Maha*. What is that again? It is the Self—the word *ātmā* (Self) being derived from the root *āp* in the sense of encompassing; for the other *Vyāhṛtis*, comprising the worlds, gods, the Vedas, and the vital forces, are encompassed by the Self in the form of the *Vyāhṛti*, *Maha*, which is identical with the sun, the moon, Brahman and food. Therefore *anyāḥ devatāḥ*, the other gods; are the *aṅgāni*, limbs. The mention of the gods is suggestive of the worlds and other factors as well. Since all the others, viz the gods, the worlds, etc., are the limbs of the Self in the form of the *Vyāhṛti* called *Maha*, therefore, the text says that the worlds etc., are made great by the sun etc., just as the limbs are made great through the self (i.e. the trunk of the body). To become great (*mahanam*) is to grow, to develop; so *mahīyante* means (they) grow. *Ayam lokaḥ* (this world), *agniḥ* (fire), *ṛgvedaḥ* (the *Ṛg*-Veda), *prāṇaḥ* (exhalation)—these are the first *Vyāhṛti*, *Bhūḥ*. Similarly, each of the succeeding ones becomes fourfold.[1]

[1] The *Vyāhṛti* called *Maha* is the trunk or self of the body of Brahman in Its aspect of Hiraṇyagarbha, for the trunk is the main thing on which are fixed and by which are sustained the subsidiary limbs. The first *Vyāhṛti* (*bhūḥ*) forms the legs; the second (*bhuvaḥ*) constitutes the hands; the third (*suvaḥ*) is the head of the Cosmic

मह इति ब्रह्म। ब्रह्मणा वाव सर्वे वेदा महीयन्ते। भूरिति वै प्राणः। भुव इत्यपानः। सुवरिति व्यानः। मह इत्यन्नम्। अन्नेन वाव सर्वे प्राणा महीयन्ते। ता वा एताश्चतस्रश्चतुर्धा। चतस्रश्चतस्रो व्याहृतयः। ता यो वेद। स वेद ब्रह्म। सर्वेऽस्मै देवा बलिमावहन्ति ॥३॥ इति पञ्चमोऽनुवाकः ॥

3. *Maha* is Brahman (i.e. *Om*), for by Brahman (*Om*), indeed, are all the Vedas nourished. *Bhūḥ* indeed is *prāṇa*; *Bhuvaḥ* is *apāna*; *Suvaḥ* is *vyāna*; *Maha* is food; for by food, indeed, are all the vital forces nourished. These, then, that are four are (each) fourfold. The *Vyāhṛtis* are divided into four groups of four (each). He who knows these knows Brahman. All the gods carry presents to him.

Maha is Brahman. Brahman means *Om*, for this being a context of words, any other meaning is inadmissible. The remaining portion stands already explained. *Tāḥ vai etāḥ*, these above-mentioned ones—*Bhūḥ*, *Bhuvaḥ*, *Suvaḥ*, *Mahaḥ*; these *catasraḥ*, four—each individually; are *caturdhā*, of four kinds, the suffix *dha* implying mode. The meaning is that they, forming groups of four (things), become fourfold (individually).[1]

Person. The main injunction here is about the meditation on Brahman as embodied in the *Vyāhṛtis*. Then follow four other subsidiary meditations on the individual *Vyāhṛtis*, each of which is to be looked upon as identical with four things.

[1] As the moon is made of sixteen digits, so also the Cosmic Person can be imagined to be constituted by sixteen limbs. Hence by thinking on each of the four *Vyāhṛtis* as consisting of four parts, one really meditates on the Cosmic Person in His totality.

The instruction, over again, regarding those very things that were thought of before, is for the sake of making a strict rule about the sequence of their meditation. *Yaḥ veda*, anyone who knows; *tāḥ*, those—the *Vyāhṛtis* as mentioned; *saḥ veda*, he knows. Knows what? *Brahma*, Brahman.

Objection: Is it not a fact that when Brahman has been already known in (the text), 'It is Brahman, it is the Self', there should not be the statement again, 'he knows Brahman', as though It is still unknown?

Answer: No, there is no fault, since the intention is to state some speciality about Brahman. It is true that Brahman has been known as identified with the fourth *Vyāhṛti* (*Mahaḥ*), but the special fact of Its being realizable within the heart has not been known; nor are the attributes beginning with 'who is realizable through knowledge' etc., and ending with 'enriched with peace' (I. vi. 1–2) which are being presented through a relationship of substance and qualities. Therefore, with a view to speaking of these, the scripture assumes as though Brahman is unknown, and says, 'he knows Brahman'. Thus there is no defect. The idea is this: He, indeed, knows Brahman who knows It as qualified by the attributes to be mentioned hereafter. Hence the present chapter is connected with the succeeding one through a single idea; for in both the chapters there is but a single meditation. And this is borne out by an indication (*liṅga*), too. For (the results spoken in) the statement, 'He resides in fire in the form of the *Vyāhṛti Bhūḥ*' etc., (occurring in the sixth chapter) points to the unity of the meditation. Moreover, this (unity) follows from the absence of any (independent) verb of injunction, for (in the sixth chapter) there is no such imperative word as *veda* (should meditate), *upāsitavyaḥ* (is to be meditated on).[1] And again, since in the chapter dealing with the *Vyāhṛtis* the statement *tāḥ yaḥ veda* (he who knows these) (I.v.3) implies something that has still to be stated, there is nothing to lead to a splitting up of the meditation (into two). And by asserting that there is an intention of stating some speciality, it has already been shown (by us) how this chapter has an ideological connection with what follows.

Asmai, to this one—who has known thus: *sarve devāḥ*, all the deities—who form the limbs; *āvahanti*, carry, bring; *balim*, offering—i.e. when 'he attains sovereignty' (I.vi.2).

CHAPTER VI

It has been said that the other deities, viz those of *Bhūḥ*, *Bhuvaḥ* and *Suvaḥ*, are the limbs of Brahman as identified with the *Vyāhṛti* called *Mahaḥ*. Just as a *Śālagrāma* (a stone symbol of Viṣṇu) is in the case of Viṣṇu, so the cavity of the heart is being presented as the place for the direct realization of and the medita-

[1] 'We do not find two independent verbs of injunction, from which to get the idea of two independent meditations. Besides, the division of the two chapters can be justified by holding one as dealing with a primary injunction and the other with a subsidiary injunction. Accordingly, there is no justification for splitting up the meditation'—Ā.G.

tion on Brahman of which those *Vyāhṛtis* are the limbs. For when Brahman is meditated on there, It is directly realized as possessed of such attributes as being 'realizable through knowledge' etc., like a myrobalan fruit in the hand. Moreover, the way to the realization of Self-identification with all has to be stated. Hence begins this chapter:

स य एषोऽन्तर्हृदय आकाशः। तस्मिन्नयं पुरुषो मनोमयः। अमृतो हिरण्मयः। अन्तरेण तालुके। य एष स्तन इवावलम्बते। सेन्द्रयोनिः। यत्रासौ केशान्तो विवर्तते। व्यपोह्य शीर्षकपाले। भूरित्यग्नौ प्रतितिष्ठति। भुव इति वायौ ॥१॥

सुवरित्यादित्ये। मह इति ब्रह्मणि। आप्नोति स्वाराज्यम्। आप्नोति मनसस्पतिम्। वाक्पतिश्चक्षुष्पतिः। श्रोत्रपतिर्विज्ञानपतिः। एतत्ततो भवति। आकाशशरीरं ब्रह्म। सत्यात्म प्राणारामं मन आनन्दम्। शान्तिसमृद्धममृतम्। इति प्राचीनयोग्योपास्स्व ॥२॥ इति षष्ठोऽनुवाकः ॥

1-2. In the space that there is in the heart, is this Person who is realizable through knowledge, and who is immortal and effulgent. This thing that hangs down between the palates like a teat—that is the path of Brahman. Reaching where the hairs part, it passes out by separating the skulls. (Passing out through that path, a man) becomes established in Fire which is (the *Vyāhṛti*) *Bhūḥ*; he becomes established in Air which is (the *Vyāhṛti*) *Bhuvaḥ*; in the sun which is (the *Vyāhṛti*) *Suvaḥ*; in Brahman which is (the *Vyāhṛti*) *Mahaḥ*. He gets sovereignty; he attains the lord of the mind; he becomes the ruler of speech, the ruler of eyes, the ruler of ears, the ruler of knowledge. Over and above all these he becomes Brahman which is embodied in *ākāśa*, which is identified with the gross and the subtle and has truth as Its real nature, which revels in the vital forces, under whose possession the mind is a source of bliss, which is enriched with peace and is immortal. Thus, O Prācīnayogya, you worship.

The word *saḥ* (he) is to be construed with *ayam puruṣaḥ* (this person), skipping over the intermediate words. *Yaḥ eṣaḥ*, this (space); that is *antaḥ hṛdaye*, inside the heart—. The heart is a lump of flesh in the shape of a lotus, which is the seat of the vital force, which opens out through many nerves, which has its stalk upwards and face downwards, and which is seen as a familiar thing when an animal is dissected. Within that is the *ākāśaḥ*, space—quite familiar like the space within a water-pot; *tasmin*, within that; exists *ayam puruṣaḥ*, this Person—who was mentioned earlier. Puruṣa is (derivatively) so called because of sleeping (*śayana*) within *puri*, the city (of the heart); or He by whom the worlds, such as the earth, are filled up (*pūrṇa*) is the Puruṣa. (He is) *manomayaḥ*: *manaḥ* means knowledge, being derived from the root *man* implying, to know; *manomaya* means 'consisting of that knowledge', because of being realized through it.[1] Or *manaḥ* may mean the internal organ (mind), being derived from

[1] Since Brahman pervades the mind. It is realized in the mind which becomes transformed as knowledge (of Brahman).

the root *man* in the sense of that through which one thinks; and one who presides over the mind, is identified with it, or is indicated by it, is *manomayaḥ*. (He is) *amṛtaḥ*, deathless; *hiraṇmayaḥ*, effulgent. A path is being indicated which leads to the realization of that Indra (i.e. Brahman) in his aforesaid nature who has these attributes, and who is realized within the cavity of the heart, and who is the Self of the man of knowledge. The nerve, called *suṣumṇā*, goes upward from the heart and is well known in the scriptures on Yoga. And that nerve runs, *antareṇa*, in the well-known middle part; *tāluke* (should be *tālukayoḥ*), of the two palates; and also through *yaḥ eṣaḥ*, that one—the piece of flesh which; *stanaḥ iva avalambate*, hangs down like a teat—between the palates. This is the idea. And *yatra*, where; *keśāntaḥ*, the ends or roots, of the hairs; *vivartate*, divide—i.e. the crown of the head; reaching that place, (the path) emerges out of it, *vyapohya*, splitting; *śīrṣakapāle*, the skull-bones on the head; *sā*, that which (thus) issues forth; is *indrayoniḥ*, the path of Indra, Brahman—i.e. the path for the realization of His true nature. The man of knowledge, who thus realizes the Self as identified with the mind, passes through the head, and *pratitiṣṭhati*, gets established; *agnau*, in Fire—(the deity) who presides over this world, who is identified with the *Vyāhṛti Bhūḥ*, and who is a limb of the great Brahman (as identified with *Mahaḥ*). The idea is that the enlightened man pervades this world through his identity with Fire. Similarly, *vāyau*, in Air; identified with the second *Vyāhṛti*, *bhuvaḥ iti*, which is *Bhuvaḥ*; 'he gets established'—this is understood. He becomes established, *āditye*, in the Sun; identified with the third

Vyāhṛti, *suvaḥ iti*, which is *Suvaḥ*. He becomes established *brahmaṇi*, in Brahman; identified with the fourth *Vyāhṛti*, *maha iti*, which is *Maha*, and of which the others are parts. Remaining in identification with them and becoming Brahman, *āpnoti*, he attains; *svārājyam*, the state of a sovereign — he himself becomes a king, a ruler over all others, just as Brahman is over the gods who form Its limbs. And the deities that become his limbs carry offerings to him just as they do to Brahman. *Āpnoti manasaspatim*, he attains the lord of the mind; since Brahman is all-pervasive, It is the lord of all the minds; indeed, It thinks through all the minds. A man who meditates thus attains It. Moreover, *bhavati*, he becomes; *vākpatiḥ*, the ruler of all the organs of speech. Similarly, also *cakṣuṣpatiḥ*, the ruler of the eyes; *śrotrapatiḥ*, the ruler of the ears; and *vijñānapatiḥ*, the ruler of intellects.[1] The idea is that he, being the Self of all, becomes possessed of the (respective) organs through identification with the organs of all beings. Besides, *tataḥ*, over and above even all that; *etat bhavati*, he becomes this. What is that? The answer is being given; (He becomes) *ākāśaśarīram* — that which has *ākāśa* (space) as its body or whose body is as subtle as *ākāśa*. Who is that? *Brahma*, the Brahman, that is being discussed. It is *satyātma*: that which has *satya*, the gross and the subtle as also truth as Its *ātmā*, real characteristic, is this *satyātma*. (That Brahman is) *prāṇārāmam*: that which has its *āramaṇa*, disport, in the *prāṇas*, vital forces, is *prāṇārāma*; or that in which the vital forces find their *ārāma*, delight, is *prāṇārāma*. (It

[1] See Ś.

is) *mana-ānandam*: that whose mind (*manaḥ*) has become bliss (*ānanda*), a producer of happiness is *mana-ānanda*. (It is) *śānti-samṛddham*: *śāntiḥ* is peace; the very entity which is peace, being also prosperous (*samṛddha*), it is *śānti-samṛddha*; or that which is experienced to be enriched (*samṛddha*) with peace is *śānti-samṛddha*. (It is) *amṛtam*, immortal by nature. These additional attributes are to be understood as belonging to the earlier context beginning with *manomayaḥ*, etc. Thus *prācīna-yogya*, O Prācīnayogya; *upāssva*, meditate on the aforesaid Brahman as possessed of the qualities of being realizable through knowledge etc. This is a presentation of the teacher's utterance by way of demonstrating his love (for meditation). The meaning of the word *upāsanā* (meditation) has already been explained.

CHAPTER VII

Of that very Brahman which has been presented for meditation as (Hiraṇyagarbha) identified with the *Vyāhṛtis*, another meditation, identifying It with the groups of five things beginning with the earth, is being stated. Because of the similarity of the number five, they are equated with the metre called *Paṅkti*.[1] Thereby everything becomes identified with *Paṅkti*. And a

[1] *Sampat* is a kind of meditation in which a lower thing is thought of as some other higher thing because of some point of similarity. Here the point of similarity is the number five. The different five factors, constituting the lower human personality, are here identified with the factors making up the higher cosmic Virāṭ.

sacrifice, too, is identified with *Paṅkti*, because the (metre) *Paṅkti* has five feet (with five letters in each), and a Vedic text says: 'The sacrifice is equated with *Paṅkti*'[1] (Bṛ I.vi.17). As a result, all things beginning from the worlds and ending with the *ātmā* (*Virāṭ*) that are thought of as reduced to *Paṅkti*, are thereby virtually imagined to be a sacrifice. Through the sacrifice thus imagined, one becomes Prajāpati (Virāṭ) who is identified with all that is equated with *Paṅkti*. As to that, it is being shown how all this Universe consists of *Paṅkti* (five factors):

पृथिव्यन्तरिक्षं द्यौर्दिशोऽवान्तरदिशाः।[2] अग्निर्वायुरादित्यश्चन्द्रमा नक्षत्राणि। आप ओषधयो वनस्पतय आकाश आत्मा। इत्यधिभूतम्। अथाध्यात्मम्। प्राणो व्यानोऽपान उदानः समानः। चक्षुः श्रोत्रं मनो वाक् त्वक्। चर्म माꣳसꣳ स्नावास्थि मज्जा। एतदधिविधाय ऋषिरवोचत्। पाङ्क्तं वा इदꣳ सर्वम्। पाङ्क्तेनैव पाङ्क्तꣳ स्पृणोतीति॥१॥

इति सप्तमोऽनुवाकः॥

1. The earth, sky, heaven, the primary quarters, and the intermediate quarters; Fire, Air, the Sun, the Moon, and the Stars; water, herbs, trees, sky, and Virāṭ—these relate to natural factors. Then follow

1 Since a sacrifice is performed with five factors—the sacrificer and his wife, the son, divine wealth, and human wealth. Thus everything can be equated not only with the metre *Paṅkti*, but also with sacrifice.

2 Some texts read it as '*vāntaradiśaḥ*.

the personal ones: *Prāṇa*, *Vyāna*, *Apāna*, *Udāna*, and *Samāna*,[1] the eye, the ear, the mind, speech, and the sense of touch; skin, flesh, muscles, bones, and marrow. Having imagined these thus, the seer said, 'All this is verily constituted by five factors; one fills up the (outer) fivefold ones by the (individual) fivefold ones.

The earth, sky, heaven, the (primary) quarters, and the intermediate quarters — these constitute the groups of five in the context of the worlds. Fire, Air, Sun, Moon, Stars — these constitute the group of five deities (lit. shining ones). Water, herbs, trees, space, and *ātmā*, constitute the collection of five natural things. The word *ātmā* implies the cosmic gross body (Virāṭ) because this is a context of natural factors. *Iti adhibhūtam*, this is with regard to natural things — this expression is used to imply the two groups of five worlds and the five deities as well, because the groups of the five worlds and the five deities, too, have been mentioned earlier. *Atha*, after that; *adhyātmam*, with regard to the personal, the three groups of five each, are being stated: Those beginning with *prāṇa* (function of exhaling) constitute the group of five vital forces. Those starting with *cakṣu* (eye) make up the group of five sense organs. Those commencing with *carma* (skin) form the group of five material constituents of the body. This much, indeed, is all that pertains to the

[1] These different forms of the vital force perform these functions respectively: exhaling, pervading, inhaling, leaving the body and digesting.

personal. And the external also is fivefold. Therefore, *etat adhividhāya*, having imagined these thus; *ṛṣiḥ*, the Vedas, or some seer endowed with this vision; *avocat*, said. What? That is being said: *Pāṅktam vai idam sarvam*, all this is verily constituted by five factors; *pāṅktena eva*, through the fivefold ones—the ones relating to the personal; *spṛṇoti*, one strengthens, fills up; *pāṅktam*, the external fivefold ones, because of the similarity of number; that is to say, they are realized as identical. The meaning is that, he who realizes all this (existence) as fivefold becomes identified with Prajāpati Himself (who is constituted by the five gross elements).

CHAPTER VIII

The meditation on Brahman as identified with the *Vyāhṛtis* was stated (I. v, vi). Then followed a meditation on the same Brahman, conceived of as a fivefold entity (I.vii). Now is being sought to be enjoined a meditation on *Om* which is involved as a factor in all meditations. For though *Om* is a mere word, it becomes a means for the attainment of the supreme Brahman or of Hiraṇyagarbha in accordance as it is meditated on with the idea of the supreme Brahman or of Hiraṇyagarbha. Just as an image is a symbol of Viṣṇu, so is *Om* verily a symbol of Brahman and Hiraṇyagarbha, in accordance with the Vedic text: '(the illumined soul) attains either of the two through this one means alone (viz *Om*)' (Pr. V.2).

ओमिति ब्रह्म। ओमितीदꣳ सर्वम्। ओमित्येतदनुकृतिर्ह स्म वा अप्यो श्रावयेत्याश्रावयन्ति। ओमिति सामानि गायन्ति। ओꣳशोमिति शस्त्राणि शꣳसन्ति। ओमित्यध्वर्युः प्रतिगरं प्रतिगृणाति। ओमिति ब्रह्मा प्रसौति। ओमित्यग्निहोत्रमनुजानाति। ओमिति ब्राह्मणः प्रवक्ष्यन्नाह ब्रह्मोपाप्नवानीति। ब्रह्मैवोपाप्नोति ॥१॥ इति अष्टमोऽनुवाकः ॥

1. *Om* is Brahman. *Om* is all this. *Om* is well known as a word of imitation (i.e. concurrence). Moreover, they make them recite (to the gods) with the words, '*Om*, recite (to the gods)'. They commence singing *Sāmas* with *Om*. Uttering the words '*Om śom*' they recite the *śastras*. The (priest) Adhvaryu utters the encouraging words with *Om*. The (priest) Brahmā approves with the word *Om*. One permits the performance of the Agnihotra sacrifice with the word *Om*. A Brāhmaṇa, when about to recite the Vedas utters *Om* under the idea, 'I shall attain Brahman'. He verily attains Brahman.

Om iti: the word *iti* (this) is used for distinguishing the word *Om* as such (and not its meaning). One should contemplate in one's mind, i.e. meditate, that *Om* , as a word, is Brahman. For *Om iti idaṁ sarvam*, all this, that consists of sound, is *Om*—since everything is permeated by *Om*, in accordance with another Vedic text: 'For instance, (as all leaves are held together) by (their) midribs, (in this way all the words are joined together by *Om*)' (Ch. II. xxiii. 3). Since all that is nameable is dependent on names, it is said that all this is *Om*. The remaining passage is for the praise of *Om*, for it is to be meditated on. *Om iti etat*, this word that is *Om*; is *anukṛtiḥ*, a word of concurrence (lit. imitation). When somebody says, 'I do', or 'I shall go', another approves the act or speech by uttering the word *Om*. Therefore *Om* is imitation (approval). *Ha*, *sma*, and *vai* indicate something well known, for *Om* is well known as a word of imitation (concurrence). *Api*, moreover; *āśrāvayanti*, (they) make them recite; with the words of direction, '*O śrāvaya iti*, *Om*, make (the gods) hear'[1]. Similarly, the singers of *Sāmas*, *gāyanti*, sing, (start singing); *Om iti*, uttering the word *Om*. The reciters of the *śastras*, too, *śaṁsanti*, intonate; *śastrāṇi*, the *śastras*;[2] *om śom iti*, by uttering the words '*Om śom*'.[3] Similarly, the priest, Adhvaryu, *pratigṛṇāti*, utters; *pratigaram*, the encouraging words; *om iti*, with the word *Om*.[4] By uttering *Om*, *Brahmā*, the priest called Brahmā (who is versed in all the Vedas and supervises the rites); *prasauti*, approves—makes them recite under direction. When told, 'I shall pour oblation', *om iti agnihotram anujānāti*, he gives

[1] The priests offering oblations get the direction from their leader thus: '*Om*, make the gods hear the formulas for oblations', and then they chant the *mantras*.

[2] The *Ṛg-mantras* set to tune are the *Sāmas*; those that are not so set are the *śastras*.

[3] *Śam* meaning bliss, changes to *śom*, in *om śom*, uttered as an acceptance of the directions of the leading priest.

[4] Adhvaryu is the priest in charge of the *Yajur-mantras*. The priest in charge of the *Ṛg-mantras* seeks his permission with the words '*Om*, may we pray?' And he replies, '*Om*, this will be pleasing to us.' Śaṅkarānanda, however, gives an alternative meaning thus: '*Pratigara* is a rite; *prati pratigaram*, with regard to this rite; *gṛṇāti*, he utters (*Om*).'

permission for the Agnihotra sacrifice by uttering the word *Om*. *Brāhmaṇaḥ*, a Brāhmaṇa; *pravakṣyan*, when about to recite the Vedas, when intent on studying; *āha*, utters; *om iti*, the word *Om*; that is, he takes refuge in *Om* for the sake of study; under the idea, *upāpnavāni iti*, may I get—I shall acquire; *brahma*, the Vedas; *upāpnoti eva brahma*, he verily masters the Vedas. Or, *brahma* means the supreme Self. (In this case the meaning is this): *Pravakṣyam*, wishing to make the Self attained; under the idea *upāpnavāni iti*, 'May I attain, the supreme Self'; *om iti āha*, he utters the word *Om*; and he verily attains Brahman by means of that *Om*. The purport of the passage is that, since the activities which are undertaken with the utterance of *Om* become fruitful, *Om* should be meditated on as Brahman.

CHAPTER IX

From the statement that knowledge alone leads to the attainment of sovereignty (I. vi), it may follow that the duties enjoined by Vedas and Smṛtis are useless. In order to avoid such a contingency, the duties are being presented here, so that they may be shown as contributory to the attainment of human goals.

ऋतं च स्वाध्यायप्रवचने च। सत्यं च स्वाध्यायप्रवचने च। तपश्च स्वाध्यायप्रवचने च। दमश्च स्वाध्यायप्रवचने च। शमश्च स्वाध्यायप्रवचने च। अग्नयश्च स्वाध्यायप्रवचने च।

अग्निहोत्रं च स्वाध्यायप्रवचने च। अतिथयश्च स्वाध्यायप्रवचने च। मानुषं च स्वाध्यायप्रवचने च। प्रजा च स्वाध्यायप्रवचने च। प्रजनश्च स्वाध्यायप्रवचने च। प्रजातिश्च स्वाध्यायप्रवचने च। सत्यमिति सत्यवचा राथीतरः। तप इति तपोनित्यः पौरुशिष्टिः। स्वाध्यायप्रवचने एवेति नाको मौद्गल्यः। तद्धि तपस्तद्धि तपः ॥१॥ इति नवमोऽनुवाकः ॥

1. Righteousness and learning and teaching (are to be practised). Truth and learning and teaching (are to be practised). Austerity and learning and teaching (are to be resorted to). Control of the outer organs and learning and teaching (are to be practised). Control of the inner organs and learning and teaching (are to be resorted to). The fires (are to be kept up), and learning and teaching (are to be followed). The Agnihotra (is to be performed), and learning and teaching (are to be carried on). Guests (are to be adored), and learning and teaching (are to be practised). Social good conduct (is to be adhered to), and learning and teaching (are to be followed). Progeny (is to be begotten), and learning and teaching (are to be carried on). Procreation and learning and teaching (are to be carried on). A grandson (is to be raised), and learning and teaching (are to be practised). Truth (is the thing)—this is what Satyavacā, of the line of Rathītara, thinks. Austerity (is the thing)—this is what Taponitya, son of Puruśiṣṭi, thinks. Learning and teaching alone (are the things)—this is what Nāka, son of Mudgala, thinks. For that indeed is the austerity; for that indeed is the austerity.

The word *ṛtam* has been explained[1]. *Svādhyāyaḥ* is study (of the scriptures). *Pravacanam* is teaching (of the scriptures), or self-recital of the Vedas (called *brahma-yajña*). These, viz *ṛta* etc., are to be practised—this much is understood at the end of the sentence. And *satyam* means truthfulness in speech, or what has been explained earlier[2]; *tapaḥ* is austerity etc.; *damaḥ* is the control of the outer organs; *śamaḥ* is the control of the inner organs. *Agnayaḥ*, the fires—are to be kept up. And *agnihotram*, the Agnihotra sacrifice—is to be performed. And *atithayaḥ*, the guests—are to be adored. *Mānuṣam* means social good conduct; that too should be practised as the occasion demands. And *prajā*, progeny—is to be begotten. *Prajanaḥ ca*, and procreation in due time. *Prajātiḥ* is the raising of a grandson; in other words, the son is to be married. Learning and teaching are mentioned in all the contexts in order to imply that these two are to be carefully practised even by one who is engaged in all these duties; for the comprehension of meaning is dependent on study, and the supreme goal (emancipation) is dependent on the understanding of the meaning. And teaching is for the preservation of that memory and for the increase of virtue. Therefore one has to entertain a love for learning and teaching. *Satyam*, truth alone—is to be practised; *iti*, this is what; *satyavacāḥ*, one whose speech consists of truth, or one whose name is Satyavacā; *rāthītaraḥ*, the teacher Rāthītara, born in the line of Rathītara, thinks. *Tapaḥ*, austerities alone—are to be

[1] See I.i: The definite ideas regarding duty imbibed from scriptures.

[2] See I. i: Righteousness reduced to practice.

undertaken; *iti*, this is what; *taponityaḥ*, one who is ever (*nitya*) steeped in austerity (*tapaḥ*), or whose name is Taponitya; the teacher *pauruśiṣṭiḥ*, who is the son of Puruśiṣṭi, thinks. *Svādhyāya-pravacane eva*, learning and teaching alone — are to be practised; *iti*, this is what; the teacher *nākaḥ*, Nāka by name; and *Maudgalyaḥ*, the son of Mudgala, thinks. *Hi*, since; *tat*, that — learning and teaching; verily constitute *tapaḥ*, austerity; therefore they alone are to be followed — this is the idea. Although truth, austerity, learning, and teaching were mentioned earlier, they are dealt with over again in order to show solicitude for them.

CHAPTER X

The *mantra* commencing with *aham vṛkṣasya rerivā* is introduced for the sake of self-recital (*japa*), and from the context it follows that the self-recital is for the sake of development of knowledge; for the present topic is concerned with knowledge, and no other purpose appears to be implied; moreover, it is considered that knowledge arises in one whose mind is purified by self-recital.

अहं वृक्षस्य रेरिवा। कीर्तिः पृष्ठं गिरेरिव। ऊर्ध्वपवित्रो वाजिनीव स्वमृतमस्मि। द्रविणꣳ सवर्चसम्। सुमेधा अमृतोक्षितः। इति त्रिशङ्कोर्वेदानुवचनम् ॥१॥ इति दशमोऽनुवाकः ॥

1. I am the invigorator of the tree (of the world).

My fame is high like the ridge of a mountain. My source is the pure (Brahman). I am like that pure reality (of the Self) which is in the sun. I am the effulgent wealth. I am possessed of a fine intellect, and am immortal and undecaying. Thus was the statement of Triśaṅku after the attainment of realization.

Aham, I—as the Self that rules from within—am; *rerivā*, the invigorator; *vṛkṣasya*, of the tree—the tree of *saṁsāra* (the world) which is subject to uprooting. My *kīrtiḥ*, fame—is high; *iva*, like; *pṛṣṭham*, the ridge; *gireḥ*, of a mountain. *Ūrdhvapavitraḥ*, I, the all-pervasive Self, whose *ūrdhvam* (cause) is the pure supreme Brahman that is *pavitram* (purifying, revealable through knowledge), am *ūrdhvapavitraḥ*. *Vājini iva* is the same as *vājavati iva*; *vājam* is food, and (*vājini* means) in one that is possessed of food—that is to say, in the sun. Just as it is a fact, well known from hundreds of Vedic and Smṛti texts, that the *amṛtam*, nectar, the reality of the Self, which is lodged in the sun, is pure; similarly, *asmi*, and I; the *svamṛtam*, beautiful, holy, reality of the Self. *Savarcasam* means effulgent; and *draviṇam* is wealth; (and) 'I am that (wealth) which is the reality of the self'—the expression 'I am' is to be supplied. Or, *Savarcasam* means the *knowledge of Brahman* which is effulgent, inasmuch as it reveals the reality of the Self; and it is called wealth, being comparable to wealth because of its producing the bliss of emancipation. On this interpretation, '(this wealth) has been attained by me', (and not 'I am') has to be supplied at the end. I, whose wisdom (*medhas*) is beautiful (*su*), characterized by omniscience, that I am *sumedhāḥ*; this fine wisdom being due to (my) being endued with the skill of preserving, creating, and destroying the world. Therefore, I am *amṛtaḥ*, possessed of the attribute of immortality; (and) *akṣitaḥ*, inexhaustible, undecaying. Or, the (latter) word may be *ukṣitaḥ*, soaked in, i.e. soaked in *amṛta*, nectar; for there is a *Brāhmaṇa* text, too; 'I am soaked in nectar.' *Iti*, thus; was the *vedānuvacanam*— the statement (*vacanam*) after (*anu*) the attainment of the realization (*vedaḥ*, i.e. *vedanam*) of the unity of the Self—; *triśaṅkoḥ*, of Triśaṅku—a seer who had known Brahman and become Brahman. This statement (of his) was for the sake of expressing the fact that he had reached fulfilment, just like Vāmadeva (Ai. II. 5). The idea is that the traditional text in the form of the *mantra*, as visualized by Triśaṅku with the eyes of a seer, reveals the knowledge of the Self. And it is understood that the self-repetition of this *mantra* is calculated to lead to knowledge. From the introduction of duty in the chapter commencing with, 'Righteousness and . . .' (I. ix), and the conclusion later on with the text, 'Thus was the statement after the attainment of realization', it becomes evident that the visions of the seers, with regard to the Self etc., become revealed to one who engages thus in the obligatory duties enjoined in the Vedas and Smṛtis, who is devoid of selfish motives, and who hankers after the realization of the supreme Brahman.

CHAPTER XI

The instruction about duties in the text commencing

with 'Having taught the Vedas', is meant to indicate that before the realization of Brahman the duties inculcated in the Vedas and Smṛtis are to be performed regularly; because the Vedic reference to post-instruction (i.e. instruction after the study of the Vedas, implied in *anuśāsti*) is meant for creating proper tendencies in a man; for in accordance with the Smṛti, 'He eradicates sin through austerities, and attains immortality through knowledge' (M.XII. 104), the knowledge of the Self dawns easily on one who has the proper mental disposition and whose mind is purified. And this Upaniṣad will say, 'Crave to know Brahman well through concentration' (III.ii). Therefore, duties are to be undertaken so that knowledge may emerge. From the mention of injunction implied in the expression, 'imparts this post-instruction', it follows that guilt will be the consequence of transgression of the command. Moreover, there is the fact of the earlier treatment of the rites etc. Rites etc. have been dealt with before the introduction of the absolute knowledge of Brahman. And this Upaniṣad will show the absence of rites etc., after the rise of knowledge, in such passages as, '(Whenever the aspirant) gets fearlessly established (in Brahman)' (II. vii), '(The enlightened man) is not afraid of anything' (II. ix). '(Him, indeed, this remorse does not afflict): Why did I not perform good deeds?' (II.ix). Hence it is known that duties are calculated to lead to the dawn of knowledge through the eradication of sins accumulated in the past. And this is borne out by the Vedic text: 'Crossing over death through rites etc., one attains immortality through meditation' (Īś. 11). The earlier inculcation of *ṛta* (righteousness) etc., (I.ix) was for the sake of avoiding the idea of their uselessness. And the present instruction is for making an obligatory rule about their performance, they being ordained for leading to the rise of knowledge.

वेदमनूच्याचार्योऽन्तेवासिनमनुशास्ति। सत्यं वद। धर्मं चर। स्वाध्यायान्मा प्रमदः। आचार्याय प्रियं धनमाहृत्य प्रजातन्तुं मा व्यवच्छेत्सीः। सत्यान्न प्रमदितव्यम्। धर्मान्न प्रमदितव्यम्। कुशलान्न प्रमदितव्यम्। भूत्यै न प्रमदितव्यम्। स्वाध्यायप्रवचनाभ्यां न प्रमदितव्यम्॥१॥

1. Having taught the Vedas, the preceptor imparts this post-instruction to the students: 'Speak the truth. Practise righteousness. Make no mistake about study. Having offered the desirable wealth to the teacher, do not cut off the line of progeny. There should be no inadvertence about truth. There should be no deviation from righteous activity. There should be no mistake about protection of yourself. Do not neglect propitious activities. Do not be careless about learning and teaching.

Anūcya, having instructed; *vedam*, the Vedas; *ācāryaḥ*, the teacher; *anuśāsti*, imparts a post-instruction; i.e. after (*anu*) the mastery of the verbal text, makes (*śāsti*) the *antevāsinam*, disciple, understand its meaning. Hence it is implied that a student who has studied the Vedas should not leave his preceptor's house without inquiring into the scriptural duties. And this is supported by the Smṛti: 'One should begin the duties after understanding them' (Āp. II. xxi. 5). How does he instruct? The answer is: *Satyam vada*, speak the truth; *satyam* is that which accords with what is grasped through valid means of knowledge and is fit to be uttered; that thing *vada*, (you) speak. Similarly, *dharmaṁ cara*, practise righteousness. Inasmuch as truth etc. are specifically mentioned, the word *dharma* (righteousness) is a generic term for all that is to be practised. *Svādhyāyāt*, from study; *mā pramadaḥ*, make no deviation. *Ācāryāya*, for the preceptor; *āhṛtya*, having brought, having offered; *priyam dhanam*, the desirable wealth, in exchange for the knowledge; and having taken a worthy wife with his permission, *mā vyavacchetsīḥ*, do not break; *prajātantum*, the line of progeny; the family line should not be broken. The idea is that even though a son is not begotten, effort should be made for his birth through such rites as the Putreṣṭi, which conclusion follows from the mention of the son, procreation, and getting a grandson (in I. ix); for, otherwise, the single word procreation would have been mentioned (there). *Satyāt na pramaditavyam*, there should be no negligence about truth. Inadvertence about truth is tantamount to falsehood. From the force of the word *pramāda*, inadvertence, it follows that a falsehood should not be uttered even through forgetfulness; this is the idea. Else there would have been a mere prohibition of untruthfulness. *Dharmāt na pramaditavyam*: Since the word *dharma* relates to practices to be undertaken, the *pramāda*, inadvertence, consists in not undertaking the practices; that should not be done.

That is to say, righteous actions must be undertaken. Similarly, *kuśalāt*, about an action meant for one's own protection; *na pramaditavyam*. *Bhūtiḥ* means *vibhūtiḥ*, welfare; *bhūtyai* about that welfare, an activity meant for welfare, about propitious work; *na pramaditavyam*. *Svādhyāya-pravacanābhyām na pramaditavyam*: *Svādhyāya* is learning, and *pravacana* is teaching; there should be no carelessness about them. The idea is that they should be regularly practised.

देवपितृकार्याभ्यां न प्रमदितव्यम्। मातृदेवो भव। पितृदेवो भव। आचार्यदेवो भव। अतिथिदेवो भव। यान्यनवद्यानि कर्माणि तानि सेवितव्यानि। नो इतराणि। यान्यस्माकꣳ सुचरितानि। तानि त्वयोपास्यानि ॥२॥

नो इतराणि। ये के चास्मच्छ्रेयाꣳसो ब्राह्मणाः। तेषां त्वयाऽऽसनेन प्रश्वसितव्यम्। श्रद्धया देयम्। अश्रद्धयाऽदेयम्। श्रिया देयम्। ह्रिया देयम्। भिया देयम्। संविदा देयम्। अथ यदि ते कर्मविचिकित्सा वा वृत्तविचिकित्सा वा स्यात् ॥३॥

ये तत्र ब्राह्मणाः संमर्शिनः। युक्ता आयुक्ताः। अलूक्षा धर्मकामाः स्युः। यथा ते तत्र वर्तेरन्। तथा तत्र वर्तेथाः। अथाभ्याख्यातेषु। ये तत्र ब्राह्मणाः संमर्शिनः। युक्ता आयुक्ताः। अलूक्षा धर्मकामाः स्युः। यथा ते तेषु वर्तेरन्। तथा तेषु वर्तेथाः। एष आदेशः। एष उपदेशः। एषा वेदोपनिषत्। एतदनुशासनम्। एवमुपासितव्यम्। एवमु चैतदुपास्यम् ॥४॥

इति एकादशोऽनुवाकः ॥

2-4. There should be no error in the duties towards the gods and manes. Let your mother be a goddess unto you. Let your father be a god unto you. Let your teacher be a god unto you. Let your guest be a god unto you. The works that are not blameworthy are to be resorted to, not the others. Those actions of ours that are commendable are to be followed by you, not the others. You should, by offering seats, remove the fatigue of those Brāhmaṇas who are more praiseworthy among us. An offering should be made with honour; the offering should not be made with dishonour. The offering should be made according to one's prosperity. The offering should be made with modesty. The offering should be made with awe. The offering should be made in a friendly way. Then, should you have any doubt with regard to duties or customs, you should behave in those matters just as Brāhmaṇas do, who may happen to be there and who are able deliberators, who are adepts in those duties and customs, who are not directed by others, who are not cruel, and who are desirous of merit. Then, as for the accused people, you should behave with regard to them just as the Brāhmaṇas do, who may happen to be there and who are able deliberators, who are adepts in those duties and customs, who are not directed by others, who are not cruel and who are desirous of merit. This is the injunction. This is the instruction. This is the secret of the Vedas. This is divine behest. (All this) is to be done thus. And (all this) must be done thus.

So also *devapitṛ-kāryābhyām*, from duties towards the gods and manes; *na pramaditavyam*, there should be no deviation; the duties towards the gods and manes must be performed. *Mātṛ-devaḥ* is one to whom the mother is a deity; as such, you *bhava*, do become; *mātṛ-devaḥ*. Similarly, you become *pitṛdevaḥ*, *ācāryadevaḥ*, *atithi-devaḥ*: the idea is that these (father, teacher and guest) are to be worshipped as gods. Moreover, *yāni karmāṇi*, those activities; which are *anavadyāni*, not blameworthy, which constitute the conduct of the good people; *tāni sevitavyāni*, they are to be resorted to—by you; *no itarāṇi*, not the others—the others that are censurable are to be shunned, though they may be followed by the good people. *Yāni*, those that are; *asmākam*, our—of us teachers; *sucaritāni*, good conduct—not opposed to the scriptures; *tāni*, those—alone; *upāsyāni tvayā*, are to be performed by you, for the sake of unseen results; that is to say, they are to be undertaken regularly; *no itarāṇi*, not the others, which are opposed (to these), though they are done by the teachers. *Ye ke ca asmat-śreyāṁsaḥ*, those who are superior to, or more praiseworthy than, us—whoever they may be—by virtue of their distinction in teachership etc.; and are *brāhmaṇāḥ*, Brāhmaṇas—not Kṣatriyas and others; *teṣām*, of them; *praśvasitavyam tvayā*, the fatigue must be removed by you; *āsanena*, by the offering of a seat etc.; *praśvāsanam* is the same as *praśvāsaḥ*, the removal of fatigue. The idea is that (their) fatigue should be removed by you. Besides (the sentence may be construed thus): *Teṣām āsane*, in their assemblage, when they are assembled for a meeting; *na praśvasitavyam tvayā*, (so much as) deep breathing should not be done by you—you should only try to grasp the essence of what they say.

Moreover, whatever is to be given, *deyam*, should be given; *śraddhayā*, with reverence; it *adeyam*, should not be given; *aśraddhayā*, disrespectfully. It *deyam*, should be offered; *śriyā*, according to (one's) prosperity. And *deyam*, it should be given; *hriyā*, with modesty; also *deyam*, it should be given; *bhiyā*, with fear; and *saṁvidā*, with *saṁvid*, which means friendly action, etc. *Atha*, then—while you are conducting yourself thus; *yadi*, if—at any time; *syāt*, should there be; *te*, in you; *karma-vicikitsā vā vṛtta-vicikitsā vā*—*vicikitsā*, a doubt, with regard to the *karmas*, rites and duties, inculcated by the Vedas or Smṛtis, or with regard to *vṛtta*, conduct, consisting in customary behaviour—; then *vartethāḥ*, you should behave; *tathā*, in that manner; *yathā*, as, the manner in which; *tatra*, with regard to that work or conduct; *te*, they—those Brāhmaṇas; *varteran*, may behave; *ye brāhmaṇāḥ*, the Brāhmaṇas, who; *syuḥ*, may happen to be; *tatra*, at that time or place; (—this is to be connected with the remote word—) *yuktāḥ*, adepts; *tatra*, in those works etc.; (the Brāhmaṇas who are) *saṁmarśinaḥ*, able deliberators; *yuktāḥ*, adepts in duties or customs; *āyuktāḥ*, not directed by others; *alūkṣāḥ*, i.e. *arūkṣāḥ*, not cruel (or not crooked) in disposition; *dharmakāmāḥ*, desirous of merit, i.e. not moved by passion. *Atha*, then; *abhyākhyāteṣu*—*abhyākhyātāḥ* are those who are charged by somebody with some doubtful guilt; with regard to them also—; you should apply all the text, *ye tatra* etc., in the way as shown before. *Eṣaḥ*, this is; *ādeśaḥ*, (the scriptural) injunction; *eṣaḥ*, this is; the *upadeśaḥ*, instruction—to sons and others by fathers and others; *eṣā*, this is; *veda-upaniṣat*, the secret of the Vedas, i.e.

the meaning of the Vedas. *Etat*, this is, verily; *anuśāsanam*, the behest of God — for the word *ādeśa* has already been explained as (scriptural) injunction. Or, *anuśāsanam* means the direction of all those who are accepted as authoritative. Since this is so, therefore, (all this) *upāsitavyam*, is to be done; *evam*, thus. *Evam u ca etat upāsyam*, and this must be done thus; this is not to be neglected. The repetition is to show regard.

Karma, Knowledge, and Liberation

Here, for the sake of distinguishing between knowledge and *karma* (i.e. scriptural rites and duties) we enter into a consideration of the question as to whether the supreme goal (emancipation) results from *karmas* alone, or from *karmas* aided by knowledge, or from *karmas* and knowledge in combination, or from knowledge aided by *karmas*, or from knowledge alone.

First opponent: As to that, the supreme goal must be the result of *karmas* alone, since a man who is versed in the full import of the Vedas is competent for *karmas*, in accordance with the Smṛti, 'The Vedas, together with their secret, are to be mastered by the twice-born.' And the mastery must be along with the purport of the Upaniṣads, which consists in the knowledge of the Self etc. Besides, in such terms as, 'The man of knowledge performs a sacrifice', 'The knowing man gets the sacrifice performed', it is shown everywhere that a man of knowledge alone has competence for *karma*. And there is the further text, 'After knowing, follows the practice.'[1] Some people verily consider that the Vedas,

[1] Seems to be an echo of G. XVI. 24.

as a whole, are meant for *karma*. Now, if the supreme goal be unattainable through *karma*, the Vedas will become useless.

Answer: No, for freedom is a permanent entity. That freedom is eternal is surely an admitted fact. It is a matter of common experience that anything that is produced by action is impermanent. Should liberation be a result of action, it will be transitory; and this is undesirable, since it contradicts the logically justifiable Vedic text, 'As in this world the result acquired through action gets exhausted, in the very same way the result acquired through virtue gets exhausted in the other world' (Ch. VIII. i.6).

Objection: Since the obligatory *karmas* are undertaken,[1] and since the works that are prompted by motives and those that are prohibited are not resorted to, and since the works that have begun to bear fruit (in this life) get consumed through enjoyment and suffering, emancipation follows independently of knowledge.

Answer: That, too, is inadmissible. For this was refuted by us by saying that, since there is the possibility of residual results of work, there lies the contingency of the production of a fresh body by them, and by saying that since the residual results of work are not opposed to the performance of obligatory duties, their elimination (by the latter) is illogical (see *Introduction*). As for the assertion that a man, possessed of the full import of the Vedas, is competent for *karma* (and that, therefore, the supreme goal must be the result of

[1] Thereby warding off all potential suffering.

karma), that, too, is wrong; for there is such a thing as meditation which is different from what is acquired by merely hearing the Vedas (at the house of the teacher). Indeed, one becomes competent to undertake *karmas* from a mere knowledge got through hearing, and he need not have to wait for meditation; whereas meditation is enjoined apart from such Vedic study (at the teacher's house).[1] And this meditation has emancipation as its result and is well known as different (from mere study). Moreover, after having said, '(The Self) is to be heard (of)', other efforts are enjoined by saying, 'It is to be thought of and meditated on' (Bṛ. II. iv. 5); and deliberation and meditation are well known (in life) to be different from the knowledge acquired through hearing.[2]

Second opponent: In that case, emancipation can result from *karma* aided by knowledge. *Karma*, as associated with knowledge, should have the power of producing a different result. Just as poison, curd, etc., which by themselves are calculated to effect death, fever, etc., can produce different results when mixed

[1] There is the general injunction about the study of the Vedas, to be sure. But the study may be merely of the verbal text or of its meaning as well. Besides, one need not know the meaning of all the texts to be qualified for rites and duties, since he can proceed to them after understanding those texts only that bear on them; the portion dealing with meditation may well be left over, since that portion is not necessary for these rites and duties.

[2] *Śravaṇa* (lit. hearing) means intelligent understanding of the import; *manana* (lit. thinking) means bringing conviction to oneself by deliberating on it and counteracting opposite ideas; and *nididhyāsana* (lit. concentrated meditation) means making it part of one's being by constant meditation.

with sacred formulae, sugar, etc., similarly, emancipation is generated by *karma* when associated with knowledge.

Answer: No, for the defect was pointed out (by us) by stating that whatever is produced is impermanent.

Objection: On the authority of scriptural text—[e.g. 'He does not return again' (Ch. VIII. xv. 1)]—emancipation is eternal, though it is produced.

Answer: No, for a scriptural text is only informative. A scriptural passage supplies information of a thing existing as such; it cannot create a thing that does not exist. Anything that is eternal cannot have a beginning, nor can anything be indestructible if it has a beginning—despite a hundred texts (to the contrary).

The third opponent answers: Hereby is refuted the view that knowledge and *karma* in their combination can produce emancipation.

Objection: Knowledge and *karma* remove the causes that hinder emancipation.[1]

Answer: No, because *karma* is known to have a different effect; for *karma* is seen to result in creation, improvement (purification), transformation, or acquisition. And liberation is opposed to such results as creation etc.

Objection: Liberation is achievable in accordance

[1] 'The hindrances are ignorance, vice, etc. Knowledge and *karma* remove them; but they do not produce emancipation itself. Thus the continuance in one's natural state (of freedom) can be eternal, since non-existence in the form of destruction (here—destruction of vice etc.) is known to be everlasting.'—Ā.G. (See p. 7, footnote 1.)

with Vedic texts that speak of courses (that are followed by departing souls). That liberation can be acquired is proved by such texts as: 'They proceed by the path of the sun' (Mu. I. ii. 11), 'Going up through that (nerve)' (Ka. II. iii. 16).

Answer: No, because it (i.e. liberation, being identical with Brahman) is all-pervasive and non-different from the goers. Brahman is omnipresent, because It is the (material) cause of *ākāsa* (space) etc., and all conscious souls are non-different from Brahman. And hence liberation is not (an) achievable (result). A traveller has to reach a place which is different from himself. Not that the very place that is non-different from oneself can be reached by oneself. And this follows from the well-known fact of identity (of the individual and Brahman) gathered from hundreds of Vedic and Smṛti texts such as: 'That (Brahman), having created that (the world), entered into it' (II. vi), 'Know the individual soul also to be Myself' (G. XIII. 2).

Objection: This (conclusion) runs counter to the Vedic texts about courses (that the departing souls follow), and the glory (that they attain), etc. Moreover, if emancipation be unobtainable, not only will the texts mentioning courses be contradicted, it will also contradict such Vedic texts as: 'He becomes one, (three-fold, etc.)' (Ch. VII. xxvi. 2); 'Should he become desirous of the manes as objects of enjoyment, (the forefathers appear by his very wish)' (Ch. VIII. ii. 1); '(he moves about . . .) with women, or vehicles . . . (Ch. VIII. xii. 3).

Answer: No, for they (i.e. those texts) relate to the

conditioned Brahman. Women or others can exist only in the conditioned Brahman, but not in the unconditioned, according to such Vedic texts as: 'One only, without a second' (Ch. VI. ii. 1); 'Where one does not see anything else' (Ch. VII. xxiv. 1); 'What will one see there and with what?' (Bṛ. II. iv. 14; IV. v. 15). Besides, the combination of knowledge and *karma* is not possible, because of their mutual contradiction. For knowledge—which relates to an entity in which all distinction of accessories, such as the agent, get merged—is antithetical to *karma* that has to be accomplished with accessories which are opposed to it (knowledge). Indeed, the same thing cannot be visualized as being in reality both possessed of such distinctions as agentship etc., and as devoid of them. Either of the two must of necessity be false. And when one or the other has to be false, it is reasonable that falsehood should pertain to duality which is the object of natural ignorance, in accordance with hundreds of Vedic texts such as: 'Because when there is duality, as it were, (then one smells something, one sees something, etc.)' (Bṛ. II. iv. 14); 'He who sees as though there is difference here (in Brahman), goes from death to death' (Ka. II. i. 10; Bṛ. IV. iv. 19); 'Hence, the finite is that where one sees something else' (Ch. VII. xxiv. 1); 'While he who worships another god (thinking), He is one and I am another (does not know)' (Bṛ. I. iv. 10); 'For whenever this one (i.e. the aspirant) creates the slightest difference in It, (he is smitten with fear)' (II. vii). And truth belongs to unity, according to such Vedic texts as: 'It should be realized in one form only'

(Bṛ. IV. iv. 20), 'One only, without a second' (Ch. VI. ii. 1), 'All this is but Brahman' (See Mu. II. ii. 11); 'All this is but the Self' (Ch. VII. xxv. 2). Nor is *karma* possible without perceiving the difference implied by such (grammatical) cases as the Dative etc. Besides, the denunciation of the perception of difference in the sphere of knowledge is to be met with at a thousand places in the Vedas. Hence there is an opposition between knowledge and *karma*, and hence also is their combination impossible. This being so, the statement that liberation is brought about by a combination of knowledge and *karma* is not justifiable.

Objection: (On such an assumption) there is a contradiction of the Vedas, for *karmas* are enjoined (by them). If like the knowledge of the rope etc., meant for eradicating the false knowledge of the snake etc., the knowledge of the unity of the Self is inculcated for eradicating the distinction of such accessories as the agent etc., then a contradiction becomes inevitable, since the Vedic injunctions about *karma* are left without any scope. But as a matter of fact, *karmas* are enjoined, and that contradiction is inadmissible, since Vedic texts are all means of valid knowledge.

Answer: No, for the aim of the Vedas is to impart instruction in respect of human goals. That being so, the Vedic texts which are devoted to the communication of knowledge engage themselves in the revelation of knowledge under the belief that since a man has to be liberated from the world, ignorance, which is the cause of the world, must be eradicated through knowledge. Hence there is no contradiction.

Objection: Even so, the scriptures establishing the existence of the accessories, viz agent etc., are certainly contradicted.

Answer: No; the scriptures, assuming the hypothetical existence of the accessories, enjoin rites and duties for the wearing away of the accumulated sins of those who aspire for liberation, and also as a means for the achievement of fruits by those who hanker after results. (But) they do not concern themselves with establishing the reality of those accessories. For, the rise of knowledge cannot be imagined with regard to one who has the hindrance of accumulated sins. On the wearing away of those sins, knowledge will emerge; from that will follow the cessation of ignorance, and from that the absolute cessation of the world. Moreover, only a man who perceives something as non-Self has craving for that non-Self. And a man, impelled by desire, engages himself in works. From that follows the worldly state, consisting in embodiment etc., for the sake of enjoying the fruits of that desire. Contrariwise, for a man who sees the unity of the Self, there can arise no desire, since objects (of desire) do not exist. Besides, since desire cannot rise with regard to oneself, owing to non-difference, there ensues liberation consisting in being established in one's own Self. From this also follows that knowledge and *karma* are contradictory. And just because of this opposition knowledge does not depend on *karma* so far as emancipation is concerned. But in the matter of attainment of one's Self, the obligatory *karma* becomes the cause for the dawn of knowledge by way of removing the hindrance of accumulated sins. We have pointed out that this is the reason why *karmas* have been introduced in the present context. Thus the Vedic texts enjoining *karmas* are not at variance (with the Upaniṣads). Hence it is established that the highest goal is achievable through knowledge alone.

Objection: In that case there is no possibility of any other stage of life (*āśrama*). Inasmuch as the rise of knowledge is contingent on *karma*, and *karma* is enjoined in connection with the life of the householders, there can be only one stage of life. And from this point of view, the Vedic texts such as, 'One should perform the Agnihotra sacrifice throughout one's life', become more apposite.

Answer: No, for *karmas* are multifarious. Not that Agnihotra etc. are the only *karmas*. There exist also such practices as celibacy, austerity, truthfulness, control of the external and internal organs, and non-injury, which are familarly associated with the other stages of life, besides such practices as concentration, meditation, etc.—all of which are best calculated to serve as means for the origination of knowledge, since they are unadulterated (with sinful acts). This Upaniṣad also will declare, 'Crave to know Brahman well through concentration' (III. ii.). And since, even before entering the house-holder's life, knowledge can emerge from the *karmas* undertaken in earlier lives, and since one embraces the householder's life for the performance of *karmas*, its acceptance becomes certainly meaningless when one has already acquired the knowledge that is (held to be) the result of *karmas* (to be performed in domestic life). Moreover, since sons etc. are meant for the (attainment of) worlds, how can there be any lingering inclination for *karma* in one who has (already) desisted from all desires for these worlds — to wit, this world, the world of the manes, and the world of the gods, which are attainable through such means as sons (and *karma* and meditation) (Bṛ. I. v. 16) — who has attained the world of the Self that exists eternally, and who finds no need for *karma*? Even for one who has accepted the life of a householder, there will surely be a cessation from *karma* after the rise of knowledge and after the renunciation of everything on the maturity of knowledge — when one feels no need for any *karma*, in accordance with the indication in such Vedic texts as, 'My dear (Maitreyī), I am going to renounce this life for monasticism' (Bṛ. IV. v. 2).

Objection: This is unsound, since the Vedas are at so much pains to prescribe *karma*. The Vedas display much solicitude for such *karmas* as Agnihotra; and *karmas* involve great effort, since Agnihotra etc., have to be performed with a variety of accessories. And since the practices pertaining to the other stages of life, such as austerity, celibacy, etc., are equally present in the householder's life, and since the other practices involve little trouble, it follows that a householder should not be placed on an equal (and) alternative footing with those in other stages of life.

Answer: No, for (the dispassionate man) there is the favourableness ensured by practices in his previous lives. As for the statement that 'the Vedas are much at pains to enjoin *karma*' etc., that is nothing damaging; for the *karmas* such as Agnihotra, as also the practices of celibacy etc., undertaken in the past lives, become helpful to the rise of knowledge, because of which fact, some are seen to be non-attached to the world from their very birth, while others are seen to be engaged in *karma*, attached to the world, and averse to enlightenment. Accordingly, in the case of those who have become detached, owing to the tendencies created in the past lives, it is desirable only to resort to the other stage of life. Since there is a profuseness of the results of *karma* — (i.e.) since there is a plethora of the results of *karma*, comprising progeny, heaven, glory of holiness, etc. —, and since people have an abundance of desire for those results, the great solicitude for *karma* evinced by the Śruti for achieving those results is reasonable: for it is a matter of experience that peoples' desires expressed in such forms as 'Let this be mine' 'May that one be mine' are multifarious. Moreover, since *karmas* are a means — (i.e.) since we have said that *karmas* are helpful to the rise of enlightenment —, one should pay more attention to the means rather than to the end.

Objection: Since enlightenment is caused by *karma*, there is no need for any other effort. If it is a fact that enlightenment emerges on the wearing away of obstacle of past accumulated sins through *karmas* alone, then apart from the *karmas*, it is needless to make any effort for the hearing (i.e. understanding) etc. of the Upaniṣads.

Answer: No, for there is no restrictive rule about that. There is surely no such rule that knowledge arises from the mere elimination of the obstructions alone, and not from the grace of God or the practice of austerity, meditation, etc.; for (as a matter of fact) non-injury, celibacy, etc. are aids to enlightenment;

and hearing, thinking, and meditating are the direct causes of it. Hereby is established the need of other stages of life, and it is also proved that people in all the stages of life can aspire for knowledge, and that the supreme goal is attainable through knowledge alone.

CHAPTER XII

An invocation is being read for warding off the obstructions to the knowledge already dealt with:

शं नो मित्रः शं वरुणः। शं नो भवत्वर्यमा। शं न इन्द्रो बृहस्पतिः। शं नो विष्णुरुरुक्रमः। नमो ब्रह्मणे। नमस्ते वायो। त्वमेव प्रत्यक्षं ब्रह्मासि। त्वामेव प्रत्यक्षं ब्रह्मावादिषम्। ऋतमवादिषम्। सत्यमवादिषम्। तन्मामावीत्। तद्वक्तारमावीत्। आवीन्माम्। आवीद् वक्तारम्। ॐ शान्तिः शान्तिः शान्तिः ॥१॥ इति द्वादशोऽनुवाकः ॥

इति शीक्षावल्ली समाप्ता ॥

This has been explained before[1] (pp. 9–12).

[1] The verbs in the second half are, however, put in the past tense. The translation of this half is: 'I spoke of you as the immediate Brahman. I spoke of you as *ṛta*. I spoke of you as *satya*. He protected me. He protected the teacher. He protected me, protected the teacher.'

PART II

On the Bliss that is Brahman

CHAPTER I

The invocation beginning with *śam no mitraḥ* was recited (at the end of the last Part) in order to avert the impediments to the acquisition of the knowledge set forth earlier. Now is being recited the invocation, *śam no mitraḥ* etc., as also *saha nāvavatu* etc., for averting the obstacles to the acquisition of the knowledge of Brahman that is going to be stated:

(For "*Śam no*" etc. see I. i.).

ॐ सह नाववतु। सह नौ भुनक्तु। सह वीर्यं करवावहै। तेजस्वि नावधीतमस्तु मा विद्विषावहै॥ ॐ शान्तिः शान्तिः शान्तिः॥

May He protect us both together. May He nourish us both together. May we both acquire strength together. Let our study be brilliant. May we not cavil at each other. *Om*! Peace! Peace! Peace!

Śam no etc., just as before, is easy to understand.

Saha nāvavatu: *Avatu*, may He protect, *nau*, us both—the teacher and the taught; *saha*, together. *Bhunaktu*, may He nourish; *nau saha*. *Karavāvahai*, may we both accomplish; *vīryam*, strength—arising from knowledge etc.; *saha*. Let the *adhītam*, study; *nau*, of us both—who are both bright; *tejasvi astu*, be brilliant;—let what we read be well read, i.e. let it be conducive to the comprehension of the meaning. There is occasion for ill-feeling on the part of the student in the matter of learning, as also on the part of the teacher, consequent on unwitting lapses; hence this prayer, 'May we not cavil' etc. is made in order to forestall this. *Mā vidviṣāvahai*, may we never entertain ill-feeling against each other. The three repetitions, *śāntiḥ*, *śāntiḥ*, *śāntiḥ*—peace, peace, peace—, have been explained already (as meant for averting bodily, natural, and supernatural hindrances). Moreover, this invocation is for warding off the impediments to the knowledge that is going to be imparted. An unobstructed acquisition of the knowledge of the Self is being prayed for, since the supreme goal is dependent on that.

The meditations relating to conjoining etc. that are not opposed to rites and duties have been stated (I.iii). After that, with the help of the *Vyāhṛtis*, has been described the meditation on the conditioned Self within the heart (I. v-vi), which (meditation) culminates in the attainment of one's sovereignty (I. vi. 2). But thereby one does not achieve the total eradication of the seed of worldly existence. Hence is begun the text, *brahmavidāpnoti param* etc., for the sake of realizing the Self as freed from the distinctions created by various limiting adjuncts, so that (as a result of the realization), ignorance which is the seed of all miseries, may cease. And the utility of this knowledge of Brahman is the cessation of ignorance; from that results the total eradication of worldly existence. And the Upaniṣad will declare, 'The enlightened man is not afraid of' (II. ix), and that it is inconceivable to be established in a state of fearlessness so long as the causes of worldly existence persist (II. vii), and that things done and not done, virtue and vice, do not fill him with remorse (II. ix). Therefore it is understood that the absolute cessation of the worldly existence follows from this knowledge which has for its content Brahman that is the Self of all. And in order to apprise us of its own relation and utility at the very beginning, the Upaniṣad itself declares its utility in the sentence, *brahmavid āpnoti param*—the knower of Brahman reaches the highest. For one engages in hearing, mastering, cherishing, and practising a science only when its utility and relation are well known. The result of knowledge certainly succeeds hearing etc., in accordance with such other Vedic texts as, 'It is to be heard of, reflected on and meditated upon' (Bṛ. II. iv. 5, IV. v. 6).

ॐ ब्रह्मविदाप्नोति परम्। तदेषाऽभ्युक्ता।

सत्यं ज्ञानमनन्तं ब्रह्म। यो वेद निहितं गुहायां परमे व्योमन्। सोऽश्नुते सर्वान् कामान् सह। ब्रह्मणा विपश्चितेति॥

तस्माद्वा एतस्मादात्मन आकाशः संभूतः। आकाशाद्वायुः। वायोरग्निः। अग्नेरापः। अद्भ्यः पृथिवी। पृथिव्या ओषधयः। ओषधीभ्योऽन्नम्। अन्नात्पुरुषः। स वा एष पुरुषोऽन्नरसमयः। तस्येदमेव शिरः। अयं दक्षिणः पक्षः। अयमुत्तरः पक्षः। अयमात्मा। इदं पुच्छं प्रतिष्ठा। तदप्येष श्लोको भवति॥१॥ इति प्रथमोऽनुवाकः॥

1. *Om*! The knower of Brahman attains the highest. Here is a verse uttering that very fact: 'Brahman is truth, knowledge, and infinite. He who knows that Brahman as existing in the intellect which is lodged in the supreme space in the heart, enjoys, in identification with the all-knowing Brahman, all desirable things simultaneously.'

From that Brahman indeed, which is this Self, was produced space. From space emerged air. From air was born fire. From fire was created water. From water sprang up earth. From earth were born the herbs. From the herbs was produced food. From food was born man. That man, such as he is, is surely a product of the essence of food. Of him this indeed, is the head; this is the southern (right) side[1]; this is the northern (left) side; this is the self; this is the stabilizing tail.

Here also is a verse pertaining to that very fact:

Brahmavit, the knower of Brahman: Brahman is that whose characteristics will be stated and who is called Brahman because of (the etymological sense of) *bṛhattamattva*, being the greatest. He who *vetti*, knows, that Brahman is *brahmavit*. He *āpnoti*, attains; *param*, the absolutely highest. That very Brahman (that occurs as the object of the verb, *vid*, to know) must be the highest (goal as well), since the attainment of something does not logically follow from the knowledge of something else and since another Vedic text, viz 'Anyone who knows that supreme Brahman becomes Brahman indeed' etc., (Mu. III. ii. 9), clearly shows

[1] *Pakṣaḥ* is interpreted as 'wing' by Ā. G. and Ś.

the attainment of Brahman Itself by the knower of Brahman.

Objection: The Upaniṣad will say that Brahman permeates everything and is the Self of all; hence It is not attainable. Moreover, one thing is seen to be attained by another—one limited thing by another limited thing. And Brahman is unlimited and identical with all; hence Its attainment—as of something that is limited and is different from one's Self—is incongruous.

Answer: This is no fault.

Objection: How?

Answer: Because the attainment or non-attainment of Brahman is contingent on Its realization or non-realization. The individual soul, though intrinsically none other than Brahman, still identifies itself with, and becomes attached to, the sheaths made of food etc., which are external, limited, and composed of the subtle elements; and as (in the story) a man, whose mind is engrossed in the counting of others, misses counting himself, though that personality is the nearest to him and supplies the missing number,[1] just so, the individual soul, under a spell of ignorance characterized by the non-perception of one's own true nature as Brahman, accepts the external non-Selves, such as the

[1] Ten men, after crossing a river, were faced with the question, 'Have we lost one of us in the stream?' So they went on counting themselves. But each one missed taking himself into account and concluded that they were only nine, one having actually been drowned. They then began wailing, when a passerby found out their foolishness, counted them one by one, and then turning to the last counter said, 'You are the tenth.' That reassured them.

body composed of food, as the Self, and as a consequence, begins to think, 'I am none other than those non-Selves composed of food etc.' In this way, even though Brahman is one's Self, It can remain unattained through ignorance. Just as through ignorance, there is a non-discovery (in the story) of the individual himself who makes up the requisite number, and just as there is the discovery of the selfsame person through knowledge when he is reminded of that personage by someone, similarly in the case of one, to whom Brahman in Its own nature remains thus unattained owing to his ignorance, there can quite reasonably be a discovery of that very Brahman by realizing that omnipresent Brahman to be none other than one's own Self—a realization that comes through enlightenment consequent on the instruction of the scriptures.

The sentence, 'The knower of Brahman attains the highest', is a statement in brief of the purport of the whole part (II). The idea involved in quoting a *Ṛg-mantra* with the words, '*Tad eṣā abhyuktā*—here is a verse uttering that very fact', are (as follows): (First) It is sought to determine the true nature of Brahman through the presentation of a definition that is capable of indicating the totally free intrinsic nature of that very Brahman which was briefly referred to as a knowable entity in the sentence, 'The knower of Brahman attains the highest', but of which any distinct feature remained undetermined; (secondly) the knowledge of that Brahman having been spoken of (earlier) in an indefinite way, it is now sought to make that very Brahman, whose definition is going to be stated, realizable specifically as non-different from one's own indwelling Self; (and lastly) the idea is to demonstrate that the attainment of supreme Brahman by a knower of Brahman—which (attainment) is spoken of as the result of the realization of Brahman—is really nothing but identity with the Self of all, which is Brahman Itself transcending all worldly attributes. *Tat*, with regard to what has been said by the *brāhmaṇa* portion (of the Upaniṣad); *eṣā*, this *Ṛk* (*mantra*); is *abhyuktā*, uttered—.

The sentence *satyam jñānam anantam brahma*—Brahman is truth, knowledge, infinite—is meant as a definition of Brahman. For the three words beginning with *satya* are meant to distinguish Brahman which is the substantive. And from the fact that Brahman is intended to be spoken of as the thing to be known, it follows that Brahman is the substantive. Since Brahman is sought to be presented as the chief object of knowledge, the knowable must be the substantive. And just because (Brahman and *satya* etc.) are related as the substantive and its attributes, the words beginning with *satya* have the same case-ending, and they stand in apposition. Brahman, being qualified by the three adjectives, *satya* etc., is marked out from other nouns. Thus, indeed, does a thing become known when it is differentiated from others; as for instance, in common parlance, a particular lotus is known when it is described as blue, big, and sweet-smelling.

Objection: A noun can be distinguished only when there is the possibility of its ruling out some other adjective (that does not belong to it), as for instance a blue or red lotus. An adjective is meaningful when there are many nouns which belong to the same class and which are capable of having many adjectives; but it can have no meaning with regard to a single noun, where there is no possibility of any alternative adjective. There is a single Brahman, just as there is a single sun; there do not exist other Brahmans from which It can be distinguished, unlike a blue lotus that can be (marked out from a red one).

Answer: No, there is nothing wrong, since the adjectives are used by way of definition (also).

Objection: How?

Answer: Since the adjectives (here) bear only a predominatingly defining sense and not a predominatingly qualifying sense.

Objection: What again is the difference between the two relations—(1) that existing between the definition and the thing defined; and (2) that between the quality and the thing qualified?

The *answer* is: An adjective distinguishes a noun from things of its own class, whereas a definition marks it out from everything else, as for instance, (the definition—) *ākāśa* is that which provides space. And we said that the sentence (under discussion) stands for a definition.

The words *satya* etc. are unrelated among themselves, since they subserve something else; they are meant to be applied to the substantive only. Accordingly, each of the attributive words is related with the word 'Brahman', independently of the others thus: *satyam brahma, jñānam brahma, anantam brahma*. As for *satya* a thing is said to be *satya*, true, when it does not change the nature that is ascertained to be its own; and a thing is said to be unreal when it changes the nature that is ascertained to be its own. Hence a mutable thing is unreal, for in the text, 'All transformation has speech as its basis, and it is name only. Earth as such is the reality' (Ch. VI.i.4), it has been emphasised that, that alone is true that exists (Ch.VI.ii.1). So the phrase *satyam brahma* (Brahman is truth) distinguishes Brahman from mutable things.

From this it may follow that (the unchanging) Brahman is the (material) cause (of all subsequent changes); and since a material cause is a substance, it can be an accessory as well, thereby becoming insentient like earth. Hence it is said that Brahman is *jñānam*. *Jñāna* means knowledge, consciousness. The word *jñāna* conveys the abstract notion of the verb (*jñā, to know*); and being an attribute of Brahman along with truth and infinitude, it does not indicate the agent of knowing. If Brahman be the agent of knowing, truth and infinitude cannot justly be attributed to It. For as the agent of knowing, It becomes changeful; and, as such, how can It be true and infinite? That, indeed, is infinite which is not separated from anything. If it be the agent of knowing, It becomes delimited by the knowable and the knowledge, and hence there cannot be infinitude, in accordance with another Vedic text: 'The Infinite is that where one does not understand anything else. Hence, the finite is that where one understands something else' (Ch. VII.xxiv.1).

Objection: From the denial of particulars in the (above) statement, 'One does not understand anything else', it follows that one *knows* the Self.

Answer: No, for the sentence is intended to enunciate a definition of the Infinite. The sentence, 'in which one does not see anything else' etc., is devoted wholly to the presentation of the distinguishing characteristics of Brahman. Recognizing the well-known principle that one sees something that is different from oneself, the nature of the Infinite is expressed in that text by declaring that the Infinite is that in which that kind of action does not exist. Thus, since the expression, 'anything else', is used (in the above sentence) for obviating the recognized fact of duality, the sentence is not intended to prove the existence of action (the act of knowing) in one's self. And since there is no split in one's Self, cognition is impossible (in It). Moreover, if the Self be a knowable, there will remain no one else (as a knower) to know It, since the Self is already postulated as the knowable.

Objection: The same self can exist both as the knower and the known.

Answer: No, this cannot be simultaneously, since the Self is without parts. A featureless (indivisible) thing cannot simultaneously be both the knower and the known. Moreover, if the Self can be cognized in the sense that a pot is, (scriptural) instruction about Its knowledge becomes useless. For if an object is already familiar, just as a pot for instance is, the (Vedic) instruction about knowing it can have no meaning. Hence if the Self be a knower, It cannot reasonably be infinite. Besides, if It has such distinctive attributes as becoming the agent of knowing, It cannot logically be pure existence. And pure existence is truth, according to another Vedic text, 'That is Truth' (Ch. VI.viii.7). Therefore the word *jñāna* (knowledge), having been used adjectivally along with truth and infinitude, is derived in the cognate sense of the verb, and it is used to form the phrase, *jñānam brahma* (Brahman is knowledge), in order to rule out (from Brahman) any relationship[1] between noun and verb as that of an agent etc., as also for denying non-consciousness like that of earth etc.

From the phrase, *jñānam brahma*, it may follow that Brahman is limited, for human knowledge is seen to be finite. Hence, in order to obviate this, the text says, *anantam*, infinite.

Objection: Since the words, *satya* (truth) etc., are meant only for negating such qualities as untruth, and since the substantive Brahman is not a well-known entity like a lotus, the sentence beginning with *satya* has nothing but a non-entity as its content, just as it is the case with the sentence, 'Having bathed in the water of the mirage, and having put a crown of sky-flowers on his head, there goes the son of a barren woman, armed with a bow made of a hare's horn.'

Answer: No, for the sentence is meant as a definition. And we said that even though *satya* etc. are attributive words, their chief aim is to define. Since a sentence, stating the differentia of a non-existing substantive, is useless, and since the present sentence is meant to define, it does not, in our opinion, relate to a non-entity. Should even *satya* etc. have an adjectival sense, they certainly do not give up their own meanings.[2] If

[1] A noun may be related with a verb by way of becoming the agent, object, instrument, receiver, possessor, or locus.

[2] 'Etymologically, the word *satya* indicates an existing entity that is not sublated; the word *jñāna* means the self-revealing cognition

the words *satya* etc. mean a non-entity, they cannot logically distinguish their substantive. But if they are meaningful, as having the senses of truth etc., they can justifiably differentiate their substantive Brahman from other substantives that are possessed of opposite qualities. And the word Brahman, too, has its own individual meaning.[1] Among these words, the word *ananta* becomes an adjective by way of negating finitude; whereas the words *satya* and *jñāna* become adjectives even while imparting their own (positive) senses (to the substantive).

Since in the text, 'From that Brahman indeed which is this Self, (was produced this space)' (II. i. 1), the word Self (*ātmā*) is used with regard to Brahman Itself, it follows that Brahman is the Self of the cognizing individual; and this is supported by the text, 'He attains this Self made of bliss' (II. viii. 5), where Brahman is shown to be the Self. Moreover, it is Brahman which has entered (into men); the text, 'having created that, (He) entered into that very thing' (II. vi), shows the entry of that very Brahman into the body as the individual soul. Hence the cognizer, in his essential nature, is Brahman.

Objection: If thus Brahman be the Self, It becomes

---

of things; and the word *ananta* is used with regard to something pervasive, as (in the expression) "the sky is infinite", etc. Hence they negate opposite ideas by the very fact of their imparting their own meanings to the substantives. Therefore they cannot be reduced to mere negation.'—Ā.G.

[1] Derived from the root *bṛh*, having the sense of growth, vastness, Brahman is that which is not limited by time, space or causation. Thus the word has its own positive import and cannot refer to a void.

the agent of cognition, since it is a well-known fact that the Self is a knower. And from the text, 'He desired' (II. vi), it stands established that the one who desires is also an agent of cognition. Thus, Brahman being the cognizer, it is improper to hold that Brahman is consciousness. Besides, that (later conclusion) leads to Its impermanence. For even if it be conceded that *jñāna* (cognition) is nothing but consciousness, and thus Brahman has (only) the cognate sense (—*knowledge*—) of the verb (*to know*, and not the verbal sense of *knowing*), It (Brahman) will still be open to the charge of impermanence and dependence. For the meanings of verbs are dependent on the (grammatical) cases (of the nouns). And *knowledge* is a sense conveyed by a root (dependent on a noun). Accordingly, Brahman becomes impermanent as well as dependent.

Answer: No, since without implying that knowledge is separable from Brahman, it is referred to as an activity by way of courtesy. (To explain): Knowledge, which is the true nature of the Self, is inseparable from the Self, and so it is everlasting. Still, the intellect, which is the limiting adjunct (of the Self) becomes transformed into the shape of the objects while issuing out through the eyes etc. (for cognizing things). These configurations of the intellect in the shape of sound etc., remain objectively illumined by the Consciousness that is the Self, even when they are in an incipient state; and when they emerge as cognitions, they are still enlightened by that Consciousness.[1] Hence these

[1] In the incipient stage, they have the fitness to be illumined; and after emergence, they remain soaked in consciousness.

semblances of Consciousness — a Consciousness that is really the Self are imagined by the non-discriminating people to be referable by the word *knowledge* bearing the root meaning (of the verb *to know*); to be attributes of the Soul Itself; and to be subject to mutation. But the Consciousness of Brahman is inherent in Brahman and is inalienable from It, just as the light of the sun is from the sun or the heat of fire is from fire. Consciousness is not dependent on any other cause (for its revelation), for it is by nature eternal (light). And since all that exists is inalienable from Brahman in time or space, Brahman being the cause of time, space, etc., and since Brahman is surpassingly subtle, there is nothing else whether subtle or screened or remote or past, present or future which can be unknowable to It. Therefore Brahman is omniscient. Besides, this follows from the text of the *mantra*: 'Though He is without hands and feet, still He runs and grasps; though He is without eyes, still He sees; though He is without ears, still He hears. He knows the knowable, and of Him there is no knower. Him they called the first, great Person' (Śv. III. 19). There are also such Vedic texts as: 'For the knower's function of knowing can never be lost, because It is immortal; but (It does not know, as) there is not that second thing, (separated from It which It can know)' (Bṛ. IV. iii. 30). Just because Brahman's nature of being the knower is inseparable and because there is no dependence on other accessories like the sense-organs, Brahman, though intrinsically identical with knowledge, is well known to be eternal. Thus, since this knowledge is not a form of action, it does not also bear the root meaning of the verb. Hence, too,

Brahman is not the agent of cognition. And because of this, again, It cannot even be denoted by the word *jñāna* (knowledge). Still Brahman is indicated, but not denoted, by the word *knowledge* which really stands for a verisimilitude of Consciousness as referring to an attribute of the intellect; for Brahman is free from such things as class etc., which make the use of the word (knowledge) possible. Similarly, Brahman is not denoted even by the word *satya* (truth), since Brahman is by nature devoid of all distinctions. In this way, the word *satya*, which means external reality in general, can indirectly refer to Brahman (in such expressions) as 'Brahman is truth', but it cannot denote It. Thus the words truth etc., occurring in mutual proximity, and restricting and being restricted in turns by each other, distinguish Brahman from other objects denoted by the words, truth etc., and thus become fit for defining It as well. So, in accordance with the Vedic texts, 'Failing to reach which (Brahman), words, along with the mind turn back' (II. iv. 1), and '(Whenever an aspirant gets fearlessly established in this changeless, bodiless,) inexpressible, and unsupporting Brahman' (II. vii), it is proved that Brahman is indescribable, and that unlike the construction of the expression, 'a blue lotus', Brahman is not to be construed as the import of any sentence.[1]

Yaḥ veda, anyone who knows—that Brahman, described before; as *nihitam*, (hidden) existing; *parame*

[1] Brahman cannot be comprehended through the common relationship of words and things denoted by them. Nor can It be denoted through the relationship of substance and quality.

vyoman (i.e. *vyomni*), in the supreme space (which permeates its own effect, the intellect)—in the space which is called the Unmanifested (i.e. Māyā), that, indeed, being the supreme space in accordance with the Vedic text, 'By this Immutable (Brahman), O Gārgī, is the (Unmanifested) space (*ākāśa*, i.e. Māyā) pervaded' (Bṛ. III. viii. 11), where *ākāśa* occurs in the proximity of *akṣara* (Immutable)[1]; *guhāyām*, in the intellect. *Guhā*, being derived from the root *guha* in the sense of hiding, means the intellect, because in that intellect are hidden the categories, viz knowledge, knowable and knower; or because in this intellect are hidden the two human objectives, enjoyment and liberation.

Or, from the apposition (of *guhā* and *vyoma*) in the expression, *guhāyām vyomni*, the Unmanifested space (Māyā) itself is the *guhā* (cavity); for in that, too, are hidden all things during the three periods (of creation, existence, and dissolution), it being their cause as well as more subtle. In that (Māyā) is hidden Brahman. It is, however, reasonable to accept the space circumscribed by the cavity of the heart as the supreme space, for the text wants to present space here as a part of

[1] 'The Unmanifested called *vyoma* (space, *ākāśa*) is inherent in the intellect (*guhā*), which is the effect of former. In that Unmanifested is placed Brahman. The element called *ākāśa* is not accepted here as the meaning of *vyoma*, since the element *ākāśa* cannot be called *parama* (supreme), it being an effect of Unmanifested *ākāśa*. Besides, in the Bṛhadāraṇyaka, the Unmanifested *ākāśa* and not the element *ākāśa*, occurs in the proximity of Immutable Brahman (*akṣara*)'. —Ā.G.

knowledge.[1] The space within the heart is well known as the supreme space from the other Vedic texts: 'The space that is outside the individual (Ch. III. xii. 7) . . . is the same as the space within the individual (Ch. III. xii. 8) (and that again) is the same as the space within the heart' (Ch. III. xii. 9). (Thus the meaning of the sentence is:) Within the cavity that is the intellect, which is within the space defined by the heart, is *nihitam*, lodged, placed, Brahman; in other words, Brahman is perceived clearly through the function of that intellect; for apart from this perception, Brahman can have no connection, (in the sense of being lodged in), with any particular time or space, Brahman being all-pervasive and beyond all distinctions.

Saḥ, he, one who has known Brahman thus—what does he do? The answer is—*aśnute*, he enjoys; *sarvān*, all without any exception; *kāmān*, desires, i.e. all enjoyable things. Does he enjoy the sons, heavens, etc. in sequence as we do? The text says: No; he enjoys all the desirable things, which get focussed into a single moment, *saha*, simultaneously—through a single perception which is eternal like the light of the sun, which is non-different from Brahman Itself, and which we called 'truth, knowledge, infinite'. That very fact is described here as *brahmaṇā saha*, in identification with

[1] Brahman is placed, i.e. manifest as the witness, in the cavity of the intellect that is lodged in the space circumscribed by the heart, and It is directly perceived there as such. If, however, Brahman is placed in the Cosmic Unmanifested, i.e. in the principle called Māyā, It will become an object of indirect perception. And an indirect realization cannot negate the direct superimposition that a man suffers from.

Brahman. The man of knowledge, having become Brahman, enjoys as Brahman, all the desirable things simultaneously; and he does not enjoy in sequence the desirable things that are dependent on such causes as merit etc. and such sense-organs as the eyes etc., as does an ordinary man identified with the worldly self which is conditioned by limiting adjuncts, and which is a reflection (of the supreme Self) like that of the sun on water. How then does he enjoy? As identified with the eternal Brahman which is omniscient, all-pervasive, and the Self of all, he enjoys simultaneously, in the manner described above, all the desirable things that are not dependent on all such causes as merit etc., and that are independent of the organs like the eyes etc. This is the idea. *Vipaścitā* means 'with the intelligent One, (i.e.) with the Omniscient; for, that indeed is true intelligence which is omniscience. The idea is that, he enjoys in his identity with that all-knowing Brahman. The word *iti* is used to indicate the end of the *mantra*.

The entire purport of the chapter is summed up in the sentence, 'The knower of Brahman attains the highest', occurring in the *brāhmaṇa* portion. And that pithy statement (aphorism) is briefly explained by the *mantra* (the *Ṛk* verse). Since the meaning of that very statement has to be elaborately ascertained again, the succeeding text, *tasmād vā etasmāt* etc., is introduced as a sort of a gloss to it. As to that, it has been said at the beginning of the *mantra* that Brahman is truth, knowledge, and infinite. The text proceeds to show how It is truth, knowledge, and infinite. As to that, there are three kinds of infinitude—from the standpoint of space, time, and objects. To illustrate: The sky is unlimited from the point of view of space, for it is not limited in space. But the sky is not infinite as regards time or as regards (other) objects. Why? Since it is a product. Brahman is not thus limited in time like the sky, since It is not a product. For, a created thing is circumscribed by time, but Brahman is not created. Hence It is infinite from the point of view of time as well. Similarly, too, from the point of view of objects. How, again, is established Its infinitude from the point of view of objects? Since It is non-different from everything. A thing that is different acts as a limitation to another. Indeed, when the intellect gets occupied with something, it becomes detached from something else. That (idea), because of which another idea becomes circumscribed, acts as a limit to the (latter) idea. To illustrate: The idea of cowhood is repelled by the idea of horsehood; hence horsehood debars cowhood, and the idea (of cowhood) becomes delimited indeed. That limitation is seen in the case of distinct objects. Brahman is not differentiated in this way. Hence It has infinitude even from the standpoint of substances. How, again, is Brahman non-different from everything? The answer is: Because It is the cause of everything. Brahman is verily the cause of all things — time, space, etc.

Objection: From the standpoint of objects, Brahman is limited by Its own effects.

Answer: No, since the objects that are effects are unreal. For apart from the cause, there is really no such thing as an effect by which the idea of the cause can become delimited. This fact is borne out by another

Vedic text which says that 'All transformation has speech as its basis, and it is name only. Earth (inhering in its modifications), as such, is the reality' (Ch. VI. 1. 4.); similarly, existence (i.e. Brahman that permeates everything) alone is true (Ch. VI. ii. 1). Brahman, then, is spatially infinite, being the cause of space etc. For space is known to be spatially infinite; and Brahman is the cause of that space. Hence it is proved that the Self is spatially infinite. Indeed, no all-pervading thing is seen in this world to originate from anything that is not so. Hence the spatial infinitude of Brahman is absolute. Similarly, temporally, too, Brahman's infinitude is absolute, since Brahman is not a product. And because there is nothing different from Brahman, It is infinite substantially as well. Hence Its reality is absolute.

By the word *tasmāt*, from that, is called to mind the Brahman that was aphoristically stated in the first sentence; and by the word *etasmāt*, from this, is called to memory the Brahman just as It was defined immediately afterwards in the *mantra*. *Ātmanaḥ*, from the Self—from Brahman that was enunciated in the beginning in the words of the *brāhmaṇa* portion, and that was defined immediately afterwards as truth, knowledge, infinite (in the *mantra*); (i.e.) from that Brahman which is called the Self, for It is the Self of all, according to another Vedic text, 'It is truth, It is the Self' (Ch. VI. viii–xvi). Hence Brahman is the Self. From that Brahman which is identical with the Self, *ākāśaḥ*, space; *sambhūtaḥ*, was created. *Ākāśa* means that which is possessed of the attribute of sound and provides space for all things that have forms.

Ākāśāt, from that space; *vāyuḥ*, air—which has two attributes, being possessed of its own quality, touch, and the quality, sound, of its cause (*ākāśa*). The verb, 'was created', is understood. *Vāyoḥ*, from that air; was created *agniḥ*, fire—which has three attributes, being possessed of its own quality, colour, and the two earlier ones (of its cause, air). *Agneḥ*, from fire; was produced, *āpaḥ*, water—with four attributes, being endowed with its own quality, taste, and the three earlier ones (of fire). *Adbhyaḥ*, from water; was produced *pṛthivī*, earth—with five attributes, consisting of its own quality, smell, and the four earlier qualities (of its cause, water). *Pṛthivyāḥ*, from the earth; *oṣadhayaḥ*, the herbs. *Oṣadhībhyaḥ*, from the herbs; *annam*, food. *Annāt*, from food, transformed into human seed; (was created), *puruṣaḥ*, the human being, possessed of the limbs—head, hands, etc. *Saḥ vai eṣaḥ puruṣaḥ*, that human being, such as he is; *annarasamayaḥ*, *consists* of the essence of food, is a *transformation* of the essence of food. Since the semen, the seed, emerging as it does as the energy from all the limbs, is assumed to be of the human shape, therefore the one that is born from it should also have the human shape; for in all classes of beings, the offsprings are seen to be formed after the fathers.

Objection: Since all beings without exception are modifications of the essence of food and since all are equally descendants of Brahmā, why is man alone specified?

Answer: Because of his pre-eminence.

Objection: In what, again, does the pre-eminence consist?

Answer: In his competence for *karma* and knowledge. For man alone, who is desirous (of results) and possessed of learning and capacity, is qualified for rites and duties as also for knowledge, by virtue of his ability, craving (for results), and non-indifference (to results). (This is proved) by the evidence of another Vedic text: 'In man alone is the Self most manifest, for he is the best endowed with intelligence. He speaks what he knows, he sees what he knows; he knows what will happen tomorrow; he knows the higher and lower worlds; he aspires to achieve immortality through mortal things. He is thus endowed (with discrimination), while other beings have consciousness of hunger and thirst only' (Ai. Ā. II. iii. 2. 5) etc.

The intention here is to make that very human being enter into the inmost Brahman through knowledge. But his intellect, that thinks of the outer particular forms, which are not selves, as selves, cannot without the support of some distinct object, be suddenly made contentless and engaged in the thoughts of the inmost indwelling Self. Therefore, on the analogy of the moon on the bough,[1] the text takes the help of a fiction that has an affinity with the identification of the Self and the perceived body; and leading thereby the intellect inward, the text says, *tasya idam eva śiraḥ*: *tasya*, of that human being who is such and who is a modification of the essence of food, *idam eva śiraḥ*, this is verily the head

[1] Though the moon is far away, it is at times spoken of as 'the moon on the bough', because she appears to be near it. The point is that, the idea of something which escapes ordinary comprehension is sought to be communicated with the help of something more tangible, though, in reality, the two are entirely disparate.

—that is well known. The text, 'This is verily the head', is stated lest somebody should think that the head is to be imagined here just as it is in the case of the vital body etc., where things that are not heads are imagined to be so. Similar is the construction in the case of the side etc. *Ayam*, this, the right hand of a man facing east; is the *dakṣiṇaḥ pakṣaḥ*, the southern side. *Ayam*, this—the left hand; is the *uttaraḥ pakṣaḥ*, the northern side. *Ayam*, this—the middle portion (trunk) of the body; is the *ātmā*, self, soul of the limbs, in accordance with the Vedic text, 'The middle of these limbs is verily their soul'. *Idam*, this—the portion of the body below the navel; is the *puccham pratiṣṭhā*, the tail that stabilizes. *Pratiṣṭhā* derivatively means that by which one remains in position. The *puccha* (here) is that which is comparable to a tail, on the analogy of hanging down, as does the tail of a cow. On this pattern is established the symbolism in the case of the succeeding vital body etc., just as an image takes its shape from molten copper poured into a crucible. *Tat api*, as to that also, illustrative of that very idea contained in the *brāhmaṇa* portion; *eṣaḥ bhavati ślokaḥ*, here occurs a verse—which presents the self made of food.

CHAPTER II

अन्नाद्वै प्रजाः प्रजायन्ते । याः काश्च पृथिवीꣳ श्रिताः ।
अथो अन्नेनैव जीवन्ति । अथैनदपि यन्त्यन्ततः ।
अन्नꣳ हि भूतानां ज्येष्ठम् । तस्मात् सर्वौषधमुच्यते ।

सर्वं वै तेऽन्नमाप्नुवन्ति। येऽन्नं ब्रह्मोपासते।
अन्नꣳ हि भूतानां ज्येष्ठम्। तस्मात् सर्वौषधमुच्यते।
अन्नाद् भूतानि जायन्ते। जातान्यन्नेन वर्धन्ते।
अद्यतेऽत्ति च भूतानि। तस्मादन्नं तदुच्यत इति।

तस्माद्वा एतस्मादन्नरसमयात्। अन्योऽन्तर आत्मा प्राणमयः। तेनैष पूर्णः। स वा एष पुरुषविध एव। तस्य पुरुषविधताम्। अन्वयं पुरुषविधः। तस्य प्राण एव शिरः। व्यानो दक्षिणः पक्षः। अपान उत्तरः पक्षः। आकाश आत्मा। पृथिवी पुच्छं प्रतिष्ठा। तदप्येष श्लोको भवति॥१॥ इति द्वितीयोऽनुवाकः॥

1. All beings that rest on the earth are born verily from food. Besides, they live on food, and at the end, they get merged in food. Food was verily born before all creatures; therefore it is called the medicine for all. Those who worship food as Brahman acquire all the food. Food was verily born before all creatures; therefore it is called the medicine for all. Creatures are born of food; being born, they grow by food. Since it is eaten and it eats the creatures, therefore it is called food.

As compared with this self made of the essence of food, as said before, there is another inner self which is made of air. By that is this one filled. That (self) which is this, is also verily of the human form. Its human form takes after the human form of that (earlier one). Of this, *prāṇa* is indeed the head, *vyāna* is the right side, *apāna* is the left side, space is the self, the earth is the tail that stabilizes. Pertaining to that also is this (following) verse:

Annāt, from food—transformed into the state of chyle etc.; *prajāḥ*, the living beings—moving or stationary; *prajāyante*, take birth; (the living beings), *yāḥ kāḥ ca*, whichever (they be)—without distinction; who, *pṛthivīm śritāḥ*, rest on, have taken as their resort, the earth—all of them are verily born from food. The word *vai* is used for calling up to memory (something mentioned earlier). *Atho*, moreover, when born; *annena eva*, by food, indeed; they *jīvanti*, live—preserve their lives, i.e. grow. *Atha*, besides; *antataḥ*, at the end, at the conclusion of the growth that is indicative of life; *apiyanti*, (they) move towards—the prefix *api* being used in the sense of towards; *enat*, it, i.e. food; the idea is that they get absorbed advancing in the direction of food, (and culminating in food). Why? *Hi*, since; *annam*, food; is *jyeṣṭham*, the first born; *bhūtānām*, of all beings. Since food is the source of all the other creatures beginning with those made of food, therefore all living beings originate from food, live on food, and merge into food. Since this is so, *tasmāt*, therefore; food is *ucyate*, called; *sarvauṣadham*, a medicine for all, a curative that alleviates the bodily discomfort of all creatures. The goal achieved by the knower of food as Brahman is being stated: *Te*, they; *āpnuvanti*, acquire; *sarvam vai annam*, all the food. Who? *Ye*, those who; *upāsate*, meditate on; *annam brahma*, food as Brahman—as shown earlier. How? Thus: 'I am born of food, am identical with food, and merge in food. Therefore food is Brahman.' How, again, does the meditation on food, as identical with oneself, result in the acquisition of all the food? The answer is: *Hi annam jyeṣṭham bhūtānām*, since food is the first born of all beings—since it is the eldest, being born before all the creatures; *tasmāt sarvauṣadham ucyate* (see *ante*). Therefore it is logical that one who worships all food as identical with oneself should acquire all food. The repetition of '*annāt bhūtāni jāyante*, from food originate all creatures; *jātāni annena vardhante*, when born they grow through food' is for the sake of summing up. The etymology of the word *anna* is now being shown. Since food is *adyate*, eaten, by creatures; and itself *atti*, eats; *bhūtāni*, the creatures; *tasmāt*, therefore—by virtue of being eaten by creatures and of eating the creatures; *tat annam ucyate*, it is called food. The word *iti* is to indicate the end of the first sheath.

The scripture starts with the text *tasmāt vā etasmāt annarasamayāt* etc., with a view to revealing, through knowledge, Brahman—which is the inmost of all the selves beginning from the physical sheath and ending with the blissful one—as the indwelling Self, by following a process of eliminating the five sheaths just as rice is extracted from the grain called *kodrava* that has many husks. *Tasmāt vai etasmāt*, as compared with this body made of the essence of food, as described above; there is *anyaḥ*, another, separate *ātmā*, self; *antaraḥ*, which is inside, (which is) imagined through ignorance to be a self, just as the physical body is; (which latter self is) *prāṇamayaḥ*: *prāṇa* is air (vital force), and *prāṇamaya* means constituted by air, possessed predominantly of air. *Tena*, by that airy (vital) self; *pūrṇaḥ*, is filled; *eṣaḥ*, this one—the self constituted by the essence of food, just as a bellow is filled with air. *Saḥ vai eṣaḥ*, that (self) which is this—the vital self; is *puruṣavidhaḥ eva*, also of a human form—

possessing a head, sides, etc. Is it so naturally? The text says, no. Now then, the self constituted by the essence of food is well known to have a human shape; *anu*, in accordance with; *puruṣavidhatām tasya*, the human shape of that self, constituted by the essence of food; *ayam*, this, (the self) constituted by air; is *puruṣavidhaḥ*, humanly shaped—like an image cast in a crucible, but not naturally. Similarly, the succeeding selves become human in shape in accordance with the human shapes of the preceding ones; and the earlier ones are filled up by the succeeding ones. How, again, is constituted its human form? The answer is *tasya*, of him, of the self constituted by the vital force, which is a transformation of air; *prāṇaḥ eva*, the special function of exhaling through the mouth and nostrils; is imagined, on the authority of the text, as *śiraḥ*, head. The imagination of the sides etc., at every turn, is only on scriptural authority. *Vyānaḥ*, the function called *vyāna* (pervading the whole body); is *dakṣiṇaḥ pakṣaḥ*, the right side. *Apānaḥ*, *apāna* (the function of inhaling); is *uttaraḥ pakṣaḥ*, the left side. *Ākāśaḥ*, space, i.e. the function (of air) existing in space as *samāna*; is *ātmā*, the self—being comparable of the Self. (*Ākāśa* means *samāna*), for it is the context of the functions of the vital force, and it is the self, being in the middle as compared with the other functions that are in the periphery. The one that exists in the middle is recognized as the self in the Vedas, in accordance with the text, 'The middle (i.e. the trunk) of these limbs is verily their soul'. *Pṛthivī puccham pratiṣṭhā*: *pṛthivī* means the deity of the earth; and this deity supports the physical vital force, since this deity is the cause of its stability according to another Vedic text, 'That deity favours by attracting the *apāna* in a man' (Pr. III. viii). Else the body would ascend upwards because of the action of the vital function called *udāna*, or there would be falling down because of its weight. Therefore the deity of the earth is the stabilizing tail of the vital self. *Tat*, pertaining to that very idea—with regard to the vital self; here is *eṣaḥ ślokaḥ*, this verse:

CHAPTER III

प्राणं देवा अनु प्राणन्ति। मनुष्याः पशवश्च ये।
प्राणो हि भूतानामायुः। तस्मात् सर्वायुषमुच्यते।
सर्वमेव त आयुर्यन्ति। ये प्राणं ब्रह्मोपासते।
प्राणो हि भूतानामायुः। तस्मात् सर्वायुषमुच्यत इति।

तस्यैष एव शारीर आत्मा। यः पूर्वस्य। तस्माद्वा एतस्मात् प्राणमयात्। अन्योऽन्तर आत्मा मनोमयः। तेनैष पूर्णः। स वा एष पुरुषविध एव। तस्य पुरुषविधताम्। अन्वयं पुरुषविधः। तस्य यजुरेव शिरः। ऋग्दक्षिणः पक्षः। सामोत्तरः पक्षः। आदेश आत्मा। अथर्वाङ्गिरसः पुच्छं प्रतिष्ठा। तदप्येष श्लोको भवति॥१॥

इति तृतीयोऽनुवाकः॥

1. The senses act by following the vital force in the mouth; all human beings and animals that are there act similarly; since on the vital force depends the life

of all creatures, therefore it is called the life of all. Those who worship the vital force as Brahman attain the full span of life. Since on the vital force depends the life of all, it is called the life of all.

Of the preceding (physical) one, this one, indeed, is the embodied self. As compared with this vital body, there is another internal self constituted by the mind. By that one is this one filled up. That self which is this, is also of a human shape. The human shape of this (mental body) takes after the human shape of that (vital body). Of that (mental body), the *Yajur-mantras* are the head. The *Ṛg-mantras* are the right side, the *Sāma-mantras* are the left side, the *brāhmaṇa* portion is the self (trunk), the *mantras* seen by Atharvāṇgiras are the stabilizing tail. Pertaining to this here is a verse:

Devāḥ, the gods—Fire etc.; *prāṇanti*, perform the act of breathing—become active through the functioning of the vital force; *anu prāṇam*, after the self that is constituted by air; that is to say, the gods perform the vital functions by becoming identified with that which possesses the power of sustaining life. Or, because this is the context of the physical body, *devāḥ* means the sense-organs; (they) *prāṇam anu prāṇanti*, become active by following the function of breathing that subsists in the mouth. Similarly, *ye manuṣyāḥ paśavaḥ ca*, those that are human beings and animals, they become active through the function of breathing. Hence, also, it is not simply by possessing the limited self in the form of the body built up by food that creatures become dowered with selves. What then? Human beings and others are endowed with their selves by virtue of possessing a vital body within each physical body, which former is common to, and pervades, each physical body as a whole. Similarly, all creatures are possessed of their selves by virtue of being provided with the bodies beginning with the mental and ending with the blissful, which successively pervade the preceding ones and which are made up of the elements counting from *ākāśa* that are the creations of ignorance. So also are they blessed with their selves by the Self that is common to all, self-existent, the source of space etc., everlasting, unchanging, all-pervading, defined as 'truth, knowledge, and infinite', and beyond the five sheaths. And by implication it is also said that this is the Self of all in the real sense. It has been said that the senses act by following the activity of the vital force. How is that so? This is being answered: *Hi*, since, according to another Vedic text, 'Life lasts so long as the vital force resides in the body' (Kau. III. 2); *prāṇaḥ*, the vital force; is *āyuḥ*, the life; *bhūtānām*, of creatures; therefore, it (the vital force) is *ucyata*, called; *sarvāyuṣam*. *Sarvāyuḥ* means the life of all; *sarvāyuḥ* is the same as *sarvāyuṣam*, the life of all. Since death is a known consequence of the departure of the vital force, the latter is universally recognized as the life of all. Hence those who, after detaching themselves from this external, personal, physical self, meditate on the inner, common vital self as Brahman with the idea, 'I am the vital force that is the self of all beings and their life—being the source of life', get verily the full span of life in this world, i.e. they do not meet with any accidental death before the ordained span of life. The word *sarvāyuḥ*, (full span of life), should, however, properly mean one hundred years, in accordance with the well-recognized fact in the Vedic text, 'He gets a full span of life' (Ch. II. xi–xx, IV. xi–xiii). What is the reason (of attaining the full life)? *Prāṇaḥ hi bhūtānām āyuḥ tasmāt sarvāyuṣam ucyate* (see *ante*). The repetition of the expression *prāṇaḥ, hi* etc., is to indicate the logic of the attainment of the fruit of meditation, to wit: Anyone who worships Brahman as possessed of certain qualities, himself shares in them.

Tasya pūrvasya, of the physical body described above; *eṣaḥ eva*, this verily is; the *śārīraḥ ātmā*, the self existing in the body made of food. Which is it? *Yaḥ eṣaḥ* that which is this one—constituted by the vital force. The rest beginning with *tasmāt vai etasmāt* is to be construed as before. *Anyaḥ antaraḥ ātmā*, there is another inner self; *manomayaḥ*, constituted by mind. *Manaḥ* means the internal organ comprising volition etc. That which is constituted by mind is *manomaya*, just as in the case of *annamaya*. This that is such is the inner self of the vital body. *Tasya*, of that (mental body); *yajuḥ eva śiraḥ*, the *Yajur-mantras* are the head. *Yajuḥ* means a kind of *mantra* in which the number of letters and feet, and length (of lines) are not restricted; the word *yajuḥ* denotes (prose) sentences of that class. It is the head because of its pre-eminence, and the pre-eminence is owing to its subserving a sacrifice directly, for an oblation is offered with a *Yajur-mantra* uttered along with a *svāhā* etc. Or the imagination of the head etc., everywhere, is only on the authority of the text. (*Yajuḥ* is a constituent of the mental sheath) since *yajuḥ* is that state of the mind which is related to organs (of utterance), effort (involved in utterance), sound (produced thereby), intonation, letters, words, and sentences; which consists of a volition with regard to these factors; which is pre-occupied with their thoughts; which has the organs of hearing etc. for its communication; and which has the characteristics of the *Yajur-mantras*. Thus are (to be understood) the *Ṛg-mantras*, and thus also the *Sāma-mantras*. In this way, when the *mantras* are considered as mental states, their mental repetition (*japa*) becomes possible, since that implies that those states alone are continued in the mind. Else, mental repetition of a *mantra* would not be possible, since the *mantra* would then be outside the mind just as much as pot etc., are.[1] But, as a matter of fact, the repetition of *mantras* has to be undertaken (since it) is enjoined variously in connection with rites.

Objection: The (mental) repetition of a *mantra* can be accomplished by the repetition of the memory of letters (constituting it).

Answer: No, since (on that assumption) there is no possibility of repetition in the primary sense. The repetition of *Ṛg-mantra* is enjoined in the text, 'The first *Ṛg-mantra* is to be repeated thrice and the last *Ṛg-mantra* is to be repeated thrice.'

That being so, if the *Ṛg-mantras* themselves be not made the objects of repetition, and if the repetition of their memory be undertaken, the repetition of the *Ṛg-mantra*, in the primary sense, which is enjoined in 'the first *Ṛg-mantra* is to be repeated thrice', will be discarded. Hence the (*Yajur*-)*mantras* are (in the last analysis) nothing but the knowledge of the Self,

[1] The words in the *mantra* would be outside the mind, and as the mind would have no independence with regard to them, there would be no mental repetition of them.

which is identical with the beginningless and endless Consciousness that is the Self lodged in and conditioned by the mental functions referred to as *Yajuṣ* that act as Its limiting adjuncts. Thus is the eternality of the Vedas justifiable. Else, if they are objects like colour etc., they will be impermanent. This is not correct. And the Vedic text, 'where all the Vedas get united is the Self in the mind'[1] (Cit.XI.1, Tai.Ā. III.ii.1), which declares the identity of the *Ṛg-mantras* etc., with the eternal Self, can be reconciled only if the *mantras* are eternal. And there is also the *mantra* text, 'The *Ṛg-mantras* exist in that undecaying and supreme space (Brahman) where all the gods reside' (Śv. IV. 8). *Ādeśaḥ* here means the *brāhmaṇa* portion of the Vedas, since (in consonance with the etymological meaning of *ādeśa*, command) the *brāhmaṇa* portion inculcates all that has to be enjoined. *Atharvāṅgirasaḥ*, the *mantra* and the *brāhmaṇa* portions seen by Atharvāṅgiras; are *puccham pratiṣṭhā*, the stabilizing tail, since they are chiefly concerned with rites performed for acquiring peace, prosperity, etc., which bring about stability. Pertaining to this is a verse, just as before, which reveals the self that is constituted by the mind:

CHAPTER IV

यतो वाचो निवर्तन्ते। अप्राप्य मनसा सह।
आनन्दं ब्रह्मणो विद्वान्। न बिभेति कदाचनेति।

[1] Where the Self exists as the witness of all mental functions.

तस्यैष एव शारीर आत्मा। यः पूर्वस्य। तस्माद्वा एतस्मान्मनोमयात्। अन्योऽन्तर आत्मा विज्ञानमयः। तेनैष पूर्णः। स वा एष पुरुषविध एव। तस्य पुरुषविधताम्। अन्वयं पुरुषविधः। तस्य श्रद्धैव शिरः। ऋतं दक्षिणः पक्षः। सत्यमुत्तरः पक्षः। योग आत्मा। महः पुच्छं प्रतिष्ठा। तदप्येष श्लोको भवति॥१॥ इति चतुर्थोऽनुवाकः॥

1. One is not subjected to fear at any time if one knows the Bliss that is Brahman, failing to reach which (Brahman, as conditioned by the mind), words, along with the mind, turn back.[1]

Of that preceding (vital) one, this (mental) one is verily the embodied self. As compared with this mental body, there is another internal self constituted by valid knowledge. By that one is this one filled up. This one, as aforesaid, has verily a human shape. It is humanly shaped in accordance with the human shape of the earlier one. Of him faith is verily the head; righteousness is the right side; truth is the left side; concentration is the self (trunk); (the principle called) Mahat is the stabilizing tail. Pertaining to this, here is a verse:

Yataḥ vācaḥ nivartante etc., (For commentary see II. ix). *Tasya pūrvasya*, of that preceding one — of the one constituted by the vital force; *eṣaḥ eva ātmā*, this one is verily the self; *śārīraḥ*, existing in the body — the vital body. Which? *yaḥ eṣaḥ manomayaḥ*, that which is

[1] Mind and speech cannot act with regard to that mental self which is constituted by themselves, since nothing can act on itself.

constituted by mind. '*Tasmād vai etasmāt*, as compared with this one' etc.—is to be explained as before—; *anyaḥ antaraḥ ātmā*, there is another self that is internal; the intelligence-self exists within the mental-self. It has been mentioned that the mental self consists of the Vedas. The wisdom about the contents of the Vedas, amounting to certitude, is *vijñāna*; and that (*vijñāna*), again, in the form of certitude is a characteristic of the internal organ. *Vijñānamayaḥ* is the self consisting of such *vijñāna*, and it is constituted by well-ascertained knowledge that is authoritative by nature. For sacrifice etc. are undertaken where there exists *knowledge arising from a valid source*. And the (next) verse will declare that it is the source of sacrifices. In one who is possessed of well-ascertained knowledge, there arises first *śraddhā*, faith, with regard to the things to be performed. Since that faith precedes all duties, it is the *śiraḥ*, head, i.e. comparable to a head. *Ṛta* and *satya*, righteousness and truth, are as they have been explained before (I. ix). *Yogaḥ* is conjunction, concentration. It is the *ātmā*, self (the middle part), as it were. Faith etc., like the limbs of a body, become fit for the acquisition of valid knowledge in a man who is possessed of a self by virtue of his concentration. Therefore, *yogaḥ*, concentration, is the self (i.e. the trunk) of the body constituted by knowledge. *Mahaḥ puccham pratiṣṭhā*: *Mahaḥ* means the principle called Mahat—the first born, in accordance with another Vedic text, '(He who knows) this Mahat (great), adorable, first-born being (as the Satya-Brahman)[1]' (Bṛ. V. iv. 1). It is

[1] The Cosmic Person comprising all gross and subtle things.

puccham pratiṣṭhā, the supporting tail, since it is the cause (of the intelligence-self). For the cause is the support of the effects, as for instance, the earth is of trees and creepers. The principle called Mahat is the cause of all intellectual cognitions. Thereby it becomes the support of the cognitive self (consisting of intelligence). Pertaining to that there occurs this verse, just as before. Just as there are verses expressive of the physical self etc., that are mentioned in the *brāhmaṇa* portion, so also is there a verse with regard to the cognitive one.

CHAPTER V

विज्ञानं यज्ञं तनुते। कर्माणि तनुतेऽपि च।
विज्ञानं देवाः सर्वे। ब्रह्म ज्येष्ठमुपासते।
विज्ञानं ब्रह्म चेद्वेद। तस्माच्चेन्न प्रमाद्यति।
शरीरे पाप्मनो हित्वा। सर्वान्कामान्समश्नुत इति।

तस्यैष एव शारीर आत्मा। यः पूर्वस्य। तस्माद्वा एतस्माद्विज्ञानमयात्। अन्योऽन्तर आत्माऽऽनन्दमयः। तेनैष पूर्णः। स वा एष पुरुषविध एव। तस्य पुरुषविधताम्। अन्वयं पुरुषविधः। तस्य प्रियमेव शिरः। मोदो दक्षिणः पक्षः। प्रमोद उत्तरः पक्षः। आनन्द आत्मा। ब्रह्म पुच्छं प्रतिष्ठा। तदप्येष श्लोको भवति ॥१॥ इति पञ्चमोऽनुवाकः ॥

1. Knowledge actualises a sacrifice, and it executes the duties as well. All the gods meditate on the first-

born Brahmā, conditioned by knowledge. If one knows the knowledge-Brahman, and if one does not err about it, one abandons all sins in the body and fully enjoys all enjoyable things.

Of that preceding (mental) one this (cognitive) one is verily the embodied self. As compared with this cognitive body, there is another internal self constituted by bliss. By that one is this one filled up. This one, as aforesaid, has verily a human shape. It is humanly shaped in accordance with the human shape of the earlier one. Of him joy is verily the head, enjoyment is the right side, hilarity is the left side; bliss is the self (trunk). Brahman is the tail that stabilizes. Apropos of this here is a verse:

Vijñānam yajñam tanute, knowledge actualizes a sacrifice; for a man of knowledge executes it with faith etc. Hence knowledge is presented as the doer in (the expression) 'Knowledge actualizes the sacrifice'. *Ca*, and; *karmāṇi tanute*, it executes the duties (as well). Since everything is accomplished by knowledge, it is reasonable to say that the cognitive self is Brahman. Moreover, *sarve devāḥ*, all the gods, Indra and others; *upāsate*, meditate on; *vijñānam brahma*, Brahman as conditioned by cognition; (which is) *jyeṣṭham*, the first born—since it was born before all or because all actions presuppose it. That is to say, they meditate on that knowledge-Brahman, by identifying themselves with it. Hence, through the worship of the *Mahat*-Brahman (Hiraṇyagarbha), they become possessed of knowledge and glory. *Cet*, if; *veda*, one knows; that *vijñānam brahma*,

Brahman as conditioned by cognition; and not only does one know, but also, *cet*, if; *na pramādyati tasmāt*, one does not err about that Brahman—does not deviate from that Brahman—. Since one is prone to thinking the external non-Selves as the Self, there arises the possibility of swerving from the thought of the knowledge-Brahman as identified with one's Self; in order to bar out that possibility, the text says, 'if one does not err about that Brahman', that is to say, if one has eschewed all ideas of identity of the physical selves etc. with his own Self and goes on thinking of the knowledge-Brahman only as his Self—. What will happen thereby? The answer is: *śarīre pāpmanaḥ hitvā*, abandoning all sins in the body—. All sins are verily caused by the identification of oneself with the body. And on the analogy of the removal of the shade, on the removal of the umbrella, their eradication is possible when their cause is removed as a result of the identification of oneself with the knowledge-Brahman. Therefore, having abandoned in the body itself, all the sins which arise from the body, which are caused by the identification of oneself with the body, and becoming identified with the knowledge-Brahman (i.e. Hiraṇyagarbha), one *samaśnute*, fully attains, i.e. fully enjoys, through the cognitive self itself; *sarvān kāmān*, all the desirable things that there are in the knowledge-Brahman.

Tasya pūrvasya, of that preceding one, of the mental self; *eṣaḥ eva ātmā*, this is verily the self, that is lodged in the mental *śarīra*, body, and is hence the *śārīraḥ*, embodied. Which? *Yaḥ eṣaḥ*, that which is this; *vijñānamayaḥ*, the cognitive one.

Tasmāt vai etasmāt etc. is as already explained. From the context and from the use of the suffix, *mayaṭ* (made of), it is to be understood that a conditioned self is implied by the word *ānandamayaḥ* (made of bliss). Indeed, the conditioned selves—made of food etc.—which are material, are dealt with here. And this self made of bliss also is included in that context. Besides, the suffix *mayaṭ* is used here in the sense of transmutation (and not abundance) as in the case of *annamaya*. Hence the *ānandamaya* is to be understood as a conditioned self. This also follows from the fact of *saṁkramaṇa* (attaining). The text will say, 'He attains the self made of bliss' (II. viii. 5). And the conditioned selves that are not the Self are seen to be attained. Moreover, the self made of bliss is mentioned in the text as the object of the act of attaining, just as it is in the text, *annamayam ātmānam upasaṁkrāmati*, he attains the self made of food (II. viii. 5). Besides, the (unconditioned) Self Itself is not attainable, since such an attainment is repugnant to the trend of the passage and it is impossible. For the (unconditioned) Self cannot be attained by the Self Itself, inasmuch as there is no division within the Self, and Brahman (the goal) is the Self of the attainer. Moreover, (on the supposition that the unconditioned Self is spoken of), the fancying of head etc., becomes illogical. For such imagination of limbs, head, etc., is not possible in that (Self) which has the characteristics mentioned earlier, which is the cause of space etc., and which is not included in the category of effects. And this is borne out by such Vedic texts, denying distinctive attributes in the Self, as the following: '(Whenever an aspirant gets fearlessly established) in this unperceivable, bodiless, inexpressible, and unsupporting (Brahman)' (II. vii), 'It is neither gross nor minute' (Bṛ. III. viii. 8), 'The Self is that which has been described as "not this", "not this"' (Bṛ. III. ix. 26). This also follows from the illogicality (otherwise) of quoting the (succeeding) *mantra*; surely, the quotation of the *mantra*, 'If anyone knows Brahman as non-existing, he himself becomes non-existent' (II. vi. 1), cannot be justified, since the doubt that 'Brahman does not exist' cannot arise with regard to Brahman which is directly perceived as the self made of bliss and possessed of such limbs as joy for its head and so on. Besides, it is unjustifiable to refer separately to Brahman as the stabilizing tail in, 'Brahman is the stabilizing tail'. So the *ānandamaya* (made of bliss, or blissful) (*ātmā*, self) belongs to the category of effects; it is not the supreme Self. *Ananda* (bliss) is an effect of meditation and rites, and *ānandamaya* is constituted by that bliss. And this self is more internal than the cognitive self, since it has been shown by the Upaniṣad to be indwelling the cognitive self which is the cause of sacrifices etc. Inasmuch as the fruit of meditation and rites is meant for the enjoyer, it must be the inmost of all; and the blissful self is the inmost as compared with the earlier ones. Further, this follows from the fact that meditation and rites are meant for the acquisition of joy etc.; indeed, meditation and rites are prompted by (the desire for) joy etc. Thus since joy etc., which are the fruits (of rites and meditation), are nearer to the Self, it is logical that they should be within the cognitive self; for the blissful self, revived by[1] the im-

[1] I.e. associated with.

pression of joy etc., is perceived in dream to be dependent on the cognitive self.[1]

Tasya, of him, of the self made of bliss; the *priyam*, joy — arising from seeing such beloved objects as a son; is the *śiraḥ*, head — comparable to a head, because of its preeminence. *Modaḥ*, enjoyment, means the happiness that follows the acquisition of an object of desire. When that enjoyment reaches its acme it is *pramodaḥ*, exhilaration. *Ānandaḥ*, Bliss — pleasure in general, is the soul (trunk) of the different limbs, (i.e. expressions) of happiness in the form of joy etc., for this *ānanda*, (i.e. common Bliss) permeates them all. *Ānanda* (Bliss) is supreme Brahman; for it is Brahman which manifests Itself in the various mental modifications, when such limiting adjuncts as the particular objects like a son, a friend, etc. are presented by the (past) good deeds and the mind, freed from *tamas* (gloom, darkness, etc.), becomes placid. And this is well known in the world as objective happiness. This happiness is momentary, since the result of past deeds that brings about those particular modifications of the mind is unstable. That being so, in proportion as that mind becomes purified through austerities that dispel *tamas* (indolence), and also through meditation, continence, and faith, so much do particular joys attain excellence and gain in volume in that calm and free mind. And this Upaniṣad will say, 'That is verily the source of joy; for one becomes happy by coming in contact with that source of

[1] 'The self possessed of joy etc. is not the primary self, since it is perceived by the witness-Self in dream' —Ā.G.

joy. This one, indeed, enlivens people' (II. vii). There is also this other Vedic text to the point, 'On a particle of this very Bliss other beings live' (Bṛ. IV. iii. 32). Thus, too, it will be said that bliss increases a hundredfold in every successive stage, in proportion to the perfection of detachment from desires (II. viii).[1] Thus, speaking from the standpoint of the knowledge of the Supreme Brahman, Brahman is certainly the highest as compared with the blissful self that attains excellence gradually. The Brahman under discussion—which is defined as 'truth, knowledge, infinite' (II. i), for whose realization have been introduced the five sheaths, commencing with the one made of food, which is the inmost of them all, and by which they become endowed with their selves (being)—that *brahma*, Brahman; is *puccham pratiṣṭhā*, the tail that stabilizes. Again, that very non-dual Brahman, which is the farthest limit of all negation of duality superimposed by ignorance, is the support (of the blissful self), for the blissful self culminates in unity. (It follows, therefore, that) there does exist that one, non-dual Brahman, as the farthest limit of the negation of duality called up by ignorance, and this Brahman supports (the duality) like a tail. Illustrative of this fact, too, here is a verse:

[1] If the increase of bliss were dependent on things alone, the Upaniṣad would not have spoken of bliss with reference to a man of detachment as it does in fact in II. viii. In reality, bliss becomes higher in proportion as the heart becomes purer, calm, and more freed from objects, whereby it becomes abler to reflect the Bliss that is Brahman.

CHAPTER VI

असन्नेव स भवति। असद्ब्रह्मेति वेद चेत्।
अस्ति ब्रह्मेति चेद्वेद। सन्तमेनं ततो विदुरिति।

तस्यैष एव शारीर आत्मा। यः पूर्वस्य। अथातोऽनुप्रश्नाः। उताविद्वानमुं लोकं प्रेत्य कश्चन गच्छती ३। आहो विद्वानमुं लोकं प्रेत्य कश्चित्समश्नुता ३ उ।

सोऽकामयत। बहु स्यां प्रजायेयेति। स तपोऽतप्यत। स तपस्तप्त्वा। इदꣳ सर्वमसृजत। यदिदं किंच। तत्सृष्ट्वा। तदेवानुप्राविशत्। तदनुप्रविश्य। सच्च त्यच्चाभवत्। निरुक्तं चानिरुक्तं च। निलयनं चानिलयनं च। विज्ञानं चाविज्ञानं च। सत्यं चानृतं च सत्यमभवत्। यदिदं किंच। तत्सत्यमित्याचक्षते तदप्येष श्लोको भवति॥१॥

इति षष्ठोऽनुवाकः॥

1. If anyone knows Brahman as non-existing, he himself becomes non-existent. If anyone knows that Brahman does exist, then they consider him as existing by virtue of that (knowledge).

Of that preceding (cognitive) one, this one is the embodied self. Hence hereafter follow these questions: After departing (from here) does any ignorant man go to the other world (or does he not)? Alternatively, does any man of knowledge, after departing (from here) reach the other world (or does he not))?

He (the Self) wished, 'Let me be many, let me be born.' He undertook a deliberation. Having deliberated, he created all this that exists. That (Brahman), having created (that), entered into that very thing. And having entered there, It became the formed and the formless, the defined and the undefined, the sustaining and the non-sustaining, the sentient and the insentient, the true and the untrue. Truth became all this that there is. They call that (Brahman) Truth. Pertaining to this, here is a verse:

Saḥ he; *bhavati*, becomes; *asan eva*, non-existing indeed—like something non-existent; just as a non-entity has no relation with any human objective, similarly, he remains dissociated from the human objective (viz liberation). Who is that? He who, *cet*, perchance; *veda*, knows; *brahma*, Brahman; *asat iti*, as non-existing. As opposed to that, *cet veda*, if he knows; That—that Brahman, which is the basis of all diversification and the seed of all activity, though in Itself It is devoid of all distinctions; *asti iti*, does exist, (then the knowers of Brahman consider him as existing). Why, again, should there be any apprehension of Its non-existence? We say that (this is so, because) Brahman is beyond all empirical relationships. The intellect that is prone to think of existence with regard to only the empirical objects having speech alone as their substance, may assume non-existence with regard to anything that is opposed to this and is transcendental. For instance, it is well-known that a pot, comprehended as a thing that man can deal with, is true, while anything of an opposite nature is false. Thus, by a parity of reasoning, there may arise here also an apprehension of the non-existence of Brahman. Therefore it is said, 'If anyone knows that Brahman does exist'. What again, will happen to one who knows Brahman as existing? That is being answered: *Tataḥ*, because of that realization of existence; the knowers of Brahman *viduḥ*, know; *enam*, this one—who has this realization; as *santam*, existing—identified with the Self that is absolutely real,—, by virtue of his having become one with the Brahman that exists. The idea is that he becomes worthy to be known by others, just as Brahman is. Or (the alternative meaning is): If a man thinks, 'Brahman is non-existence', then that man, because of his faithlessness the entire righteous path consisting of the scheme of castes, stages of life, etc., becomes non-existent inasmuch as that path is not calculated to lead him to Brahman. Hence this atheist is called *asat*, unrighteous—in this world. As opposed to such a man, if anyone knows that 'Brahman does exist', then, he, because of his faith, accepts properly the righteous path comprising the scheme of castes, stages of life, etc. and leading to the realization of Brahman. Since this is so, *tataḥ*, therefore; the good people know this one as *santam*, treading the righteous path. The purport of the sentence is: Because of this fact, Brahman is to be accepted as surely existing.

Tasya pūrvasya, of the preceding one—of the cognitive one; *eṣaḥ eva*, this one, indeed; is *śārīraḥ ātmā*, the self existing in the body made of knowledge. Which is that? *Yaḥ eṣaḥ*, that which is this one—the self made of bliss. As to this self there is no apprehension of non-existence. But Brahman's non-existence may be suspected, since It is devoid of all distinctions, and since It is common to all.[1] Since this is so, *ataḥ*, therefore; *atha*, afterwards; there are these *anupraśnāḥ*: *praśnāḥ* means questions, by the disciple who is the hearer, and *anu* means after; the questions after what the teacher has spoken are the *anupraśnāḥ*. Brahman, being the cause of space etc., is equally common to the man of knowledge and the ignorant. Therefore, it may be suspected that the ignorant man, too, reaches Brahman. *Uta* has the meaning of *api* (used in introducing a question). *Cana* is used in the sense of *api* (implying *even*). *Pretya*, departing, from here; does *kaḥ cana avidvān*, even one who is ignorant; *gacchati*, reach; *amum lokam*, that world—the supreme Self? The question, 'Or does he not go ?' is implied because of the use of the plural number in '*anupraśnāḥ*, questions put after the teacher's instruction.' The remaining two questions are with regard to the enlightened man. If the ignorant man fails to reach Brahman, though It is the common source of all, then the attainment of Brahman by an enlightened man may as well be doubted. Hence with regard to him is the question: *Āho vidvān* etc. Does *kaḥ cit*, someone; who is a *vidvān*, an enlightened man, a knower of Brahman; *pretya*, departing, from here; *amum lokam samaśnute*, reach the other world? In the expression *samaśnute u*, the *e* (in *te*) is replaced by *ay*, of which the *y* having been dropped out, the *a* becomes

[1] Since Brahman pervades everything, Its utility should be perceptible at every turn. But actually this is not so. Hence Its existence can be questioned. But the *ānandamaya*'s (the blissful self's) existence is not doubted in this sense. Hence *ānandamaya* is not the subject-matter of the verse quoted above.

lengthened, and the expression becomes *samaśnutā u*. And the letter *u*, occuring later, should be transferred from the bottom and the letter *ta* should be detached from *uta*, occuring earlier, (to form a new word *uta*). Placing this (new) *uta* before the word *āho*, the question is being put: '*Uta āho vidvān* . . . : Or does the enlightened man attain the other world?' The other question is: 'Or does the enlightened man not attain it, just as the ignorant man does not?' Alternatively, there are only two questions relating to the enlightened and the unenlightened men. But the plural occurs with reference to other questions that may crop up by implication. From hearing, 'If one knows Brahman, as non-existing', and 'if one knows that Brahman does exist', the doubt arises as to whether It exists or does not exist. From that, by implication, crops up this first question after the teacher's instruction: 'Does Brahman exist or does It not?' The second one is: 'Since Brahman is impartial, does the unenlightened man reach It or does he not?' Even if Brahman is equal to all, Its non-attainment in the case of the enlightened man can be suspected as much as in the case of the unenlightened one; and hence the third question following on the teacher's instruction, is, 'Does the man of knowledge attain or does he not?' The succeeding text is introduced for answering these questions.

Apropos of this, existence is being first spoken of. It remains to be explained as to what kind of truth is meant in the assertion that was made thus: 'Brahman is truth, knowledge, infinite'. Hence it is being said: Brahman's truth is affirmed by speaking of Its existence; for it has been asserted that the existing is the true (an echo of Ch. VI. ii. 1). Therefore, the very affirmation of existence amounts to an avowal of reality. How is it known that this text bears such an import? From the trend of the words of this text. For the succeeding sentences such as, 'They call that (Brahman) Truth' (II. vi), '(Who, indeed will inhale and who exhale) if this Bliss (Brahman) be not there in the supreme space (within the heart)?', are connected with this very purport.

Objection: While on this topic, the suspicion arises that Brahman is surely non-existent. Why? Because whatever exists is perceived as possessed of distinctive attributes, as for instance a pot etc. Whatever is non-existent is not perceived, as for instance the horn of a hare etc. Similarly, Brahman is not perceived. So It does not exist, since It is not perceived as possessed of distinguishing attributes.

Answer: This is not tenable, since Brahman is the cause of space etc. It is not a fact that Brahman does not exist. Why? Since all the products issuing from Brahman, such as space etc., are perceived. It is a matter of common experience in this world that any thing from which something is produced does exist, as for instance, earth, seed, etc., which are the causes of a pot, a sprout, etc. So Brahman does exist, since It is the cause of space etc. And, no effect is perceived in this world as having been produced from a nonentity. If such effects as name and form had originated from a nonentity, they should not have been perceived since they have no reality. But they are perceived. Hence Brahman exists. Should any effect originate from a nonentity, it should remain soaked in unreality even while being perceived. But facts point otherwise. Therefore Brahman exists. Pertaining to this another Vedic text—'How can a thing that exists come out of a thing that does not?' (Ch. VI. ii. 2)—points out logically the impossiblity of the creation of something out of nothing. Therefore, it stands to reason that Brahman is verily a reality.

Objection: Should that Brahman be a cause like earth, seed, etc., It will be insentient.

Answer: No, since It is capable of desiring. Certainly it is not a matter of experience that one who can desire can be insentient. We have said that Brahman is indeed omniscient; and so it is but reasonable that It should be capable of desiring.

Objection: Since Brahman has desires, It has unfulfilled desires like ourselves.

Answer: Not so, for It is independent. Such defects as desire cannot impel Brahman (to action) just as they do others by subjecting them to their influence. What then are these (desires of Brahman)? They are by nature truth and knowledge, and they are pure by virtue of their identity with Brahman.[1] Brahman is not impelled to action by them. But Brahman ordains them in accordance with the results of actions of the creatures. Therefore, Brahman has independence with

1 'Brahman, as reflected on Māyā, is the material cause of the world, and It is possessed of desires that are the modifications of Māyā. But these modifications are not distinguishable from truth and knowledge, since they are permeated by Consciousness that is not subject to ignorance etc.; and they are pure, since they are untouched by unrighteousness etc. by virtue of their non-distinction from Brahman.' —Ā.G.

regard to desires. So Brahman has no want. And this follows also from the fact of Brahman's non-dependence on any other means. Further, Brahman has no dependence on accessories etc., as others have whose desires are not identified with themselves but are dependent on such causes as righteousness, and require the extraneous body and senses as their instruments. How do they exist then (in Brahman)? They are non-different from Itself.[1] That fact is stated in *saḥ akāmayata*: *saḥ*, the Self from which space originated; *akāmayata*, desired. How? *Bahu syām*: *syām*, I shall become; *bahu*, many.

Objection: How can the One become many, unless It enters into something else?

The *answer* is, '*prajayeya*, I shall be born'. The multiplication here does not refer to becoming something extraneous as one does by begetting a son. How then? Through the manifestation of name and form that are latent in Itself. When name and form existing latently in the Self get manifested, they evolve—by retaining their intrinsic nature as the Self under all conditions—in time and space which are inseparable from Brahman. Then that evolution of name and form is (what is called) the appearance of Brahman as the many. In no other way is it possible for the partless Brahman to become either multiple or finite; as for instance, the

[1] 'Since Māyā, as possessed of the impressions of desires, has identity with Brahman (through superimposition), the desires, too, that are the modifications of this Māyā, have identity with Brahman. Therefore, there is no need for a physical body etc. (for making possible the existence of desires in Brahman, as it is in our case)' —Ā.G.

finitude and plurality of space are surely the creations of extraneous factors. Hence the Self becomes multiple through these alone. For no such subtle, disconnected and remote thing exists as a non-Self, in the past, present, or future, which is different from the Self and separated from It by time or space. Therefore, it is only because of Brahman that name and form have their being under all circumstances, but Brahman does not consist of them. They are said to be essentially Brahman, since they cease to exist when Brahman is eliminated. And, conditioned by these two limiting adjuncts, Brahman becomes a factor in all empirical dealings involving such words as knower, knowable and knowledge, as also their implications etc.

Having such a desire, *saḥ*, He—that Self; *tapaḥ, atapyata*: by *tapaḥ* is meant knowledge since another Vedic text says, 'He whose *tapaḥ* consists of knowledge' (Mu. I.i.9), and since the other kind of *tapaḥ* (austerity) is out of place in one in whom all desires remain fulfilled. That kind of *tapaḥ*, knowledge; he *atapyata*, practised. The idea is that the Self reflected on the plan etc. of the world being created. *Saḥ tapaḥ taptvā*, He, having reflected thus; *asṛjata*, created, in consonance with such contributory factors as the results of actions of creatures; *idam sarvam*, all this; *yat idam kim ca*, whatever there is, without any exception—this universe, together with space, time, name, and form as He perceived it, and as it is perceived by all beings under various circumstances. Brahman, *sṛṣṭvā*, having created; *tat*, that, this world;—what did He do? the answer is—*tat eva*, into that very world, which had been created; *anuprāviśat*, He entered.

With regard to this, it is a matter for consideration as to how He entered. Did the Creator enter in that very form of His or in some other form? Which is the reasonable position?

Pseudo-Vedāntin: From the use of the suffix *ktvā* (-ing), it follows that the Creator Himself entered.[1]

Objection: Is that not illogical, since on the supposition that Brahman is a (material) cause in the same sense as clay is (of pot etc.), the effects are non-different from Brahman? For it is the cause that becomes transformed into the effect. Hence it is illogical that, after the production of the effect, the cause should enter over again into the effect as a separate entity, as though it had not done so already.[2] Apart from being shaped into a pot, the clay has no other entry into the pot, to be sure.

Pseudo-Vedāntin: Just as earth, in the form of dust, enters into a pot (made of earth), similarly, the Self can enter into name and form under some other guise. And this also follows from another Vedic text, 'By entering in the form of the soul of each individual being . . .' (Ch. VI. iii. 2).

Objection: This is not proper, since Brahman is one. In the case of earth, however, it is possible to enter into a pot in the form of dust, since lumps of earth are

[1] Grammar indicates that the finite verb and the verb ending with *ktvā* (-ing), in the same sentence, refer to the same nominative.

[2] The action denoted by the verb having the suffix *ktvā* precedes the action of the finite verb. This is not possible here, since the production of the effect and the entry of the cause into it are simultaneous.

many and have parts, and since powder of earth has places still unoccupied by it. In the case of the Self, however, there cannot possibly be any entry, since It is one at the same time that It has no dimension and has nowhere to enter into.

Pseudo-Vedāntin: What kind of entry will it be then? And, the fact of entry has to be upheld in view of the Upaniṣadic statement: 'He entered into that very thing.' That being so, Brahman may as well have dimensions, and having dimensions, it is but proper that Brahman's entry in the form of an individual soul into name and form should be like that of a hand into the mouth.

Objection: No, since there is no empty space. For Brahman, which has become transformed into effects, has no other space—apart from that occupied by the effects, consisting of name and form—which is devoid of It and into which It can enter as an individual soul. Should It (i.e. Brahman as the individual soul) enter into the cause (viz Brahman as name and form),[1] It will cease to be an individual soul, just as a pot ceases to be a pot on entering into (i.e. on being reduced to) earth. Hence the text, 'He entered into that very thing', cannot justifiably imply entry into the cause.

Pseudo-Vedāntin: Let (the entry be into) another effect. The text, 'He entered into that very thing', means that one effect, viz the individual soul, entered into another effect made of name and form.

Objection: No, since this involves a contradiction;

[1] Brahman is the common cause of everything including the individual souls. Now, the individual soul may enter into Brahman which, though transformed as name and form, is still its cause.

for a pot does not become merged into another pot. Besides, this runs counter to the Vedic texts that speak of their distinction; so, the Vedic texts that reaffirm the difference of the individual soul from the effect, name and form, will be contradicted. Furthermore, if the soul merges into name and form, liberation will be impossible. It does not stand to reason that one merges into what one tries to get freed from. A chained thief does not enter into fetters.[1]

Pseudo-Vedāntin: Suppose Brahman is transformed into two parts, external and internal. To explain, that very Brahman which is the cause, has become diversified as the receptacle in the shape of body etc., and as the thing contained in the shape of the embodied soul.

Objection: No, for entry is possible only for what is outside. Not that a thing which is (naturally) contained within another is said to have entered there. The entry should be of something that is outside, for the word entry (*praveśa*) is seen to carry that sense, as for instance in the sentence, 'He entered into the house after erecting it.'

Pseudo-Vedāntin: The entry may be like that of the reflections of the sun etc. in water.

Objection: No, since Brahman is not limited, and since It has no configuration. A distinct thing that is limited and has features can be a production of reflection on something else which is by nature transparent, as for instance, the sun etc. can be reflected on water; but of the Self there can be no reflection, since It has

[1] The freedom of a thief, when captured, does not lie in his entering into the fetters.

no form. Moreover, the entry of the Self in the form of a reflection is not possible, since the Self is all-pervasive, being the cause of space etc., and since there is no other substance which can hold the Self's reflection by being placed somewhere unconnected with the Self. This being so, there is no entry whatsoever. Nor do we find any other interpretation possible for the text, 'He entered into that very thing.' And a Vedic text is meant to enlighten us about supersensuous realities. But from this sentence, not even diligent people can derive any enlightenment. Well, then, this sentence, 'Having created it, He entered into that very thing,' has to be discarded, since it conveys no meaning.

Vedāntin's answer: No, (it need not be discarded). As the sentence bears a different meaning, why should there be this discussion that is out of context? You should remember the other meaning which is implied in this sentence and which is the subject under discussion here, as stated in the text: 'The knower of Brahman attains the highest. . . . Brahman is truth, knowledge, and infinite. . . . He who knows (that Brahman) as existing in the intellect (lodged in the supreme space in the heart)' (II. i). The knowledge of that Brahman is sought to be imparted, and that is also the topic under discussion. And the effects, beginning with space and ending with the body made of food, have been introduced with a view to acquiring the knowledge of the nature of that Brahman, and the topic started with is also the knowledge of Brahman. Of these, the self made of the vital force indwells and is different from the self made of food; within that is the self made of mind and the self made of intellect. Thus (by stages) the Self has been made to enter into the cavity of the intellect. And there, again, has been presented a distinct self that is made of bliss. After this, through the comprehension of the blissful self which acts as a pointer (to the Bliss-Brahman), one has to realize, within this very cavity (of the heart), that Self as the culmination of the growth of bliss, which is Brahman (conceived of) as the stabilizing tail (of the blissful self), which is the support of all modifications and which is devoid of all modifications. It is with this idea that the entry of the Self is imagined. Inasmuch as Brahman has no distinctive attribute, It cannot be realized anywhere else. It is a matter of experience that knowledge of a thing is dependent on its particular associations. Just as the knowledge of Rāhu arises from its association with the distinct entities, the sun and the moon,[1] similarly, the association of the Self with the cavity of the internal organ causes the knowledge of Brahman, for the internal organ has proximity (to the Self) and the nature of illumination. Just as pot etc. are perceived when in contact with light, so also the Self is perceived when in contact with the light of intellectual conviction.[2] Hence, it suits the context to

1 Rāhu is a mythological being that has no limb except a head. During eclipses it swallows the sun or the moon, and then alone we are conscious of its existence.

2 A thing becomes illumined with the light of knowledge, only when the internal organ is in contact with it, but not otherwise. A reflecting medium must be transparent enough to catch an image properly. The intellect alone can reflect the Self best. Again, light removes darkness, though both are insentient, similarly, intellectual conviction removes ignorance, though both are insentient. The intellect cannot reveal Brahman objectively.

say that the Self is lodged in the cavity of the intellect which is the cause of Its experience. In the present passage, however, which is a sort of elaboration of that theme, the same idea is repeated in the form, 'Having created it, He entered into that very thing.' *Tat*, that very Brahman Itself—which is the cause of space; and which, *sṛṣṭvā*, after creating the effect, has entered into the creation, as it were, is perceived within the cavity of intellect, as possessed of such distinctions as being a seer, a hearer, a thinker, a knower, etc. That, indeed, is Its entry. Hence Brahman, as the cause of this (phenomenon), must exist. Accordingly, just because It exists, It should surely be apprehended as such.

What did It do after entering the creation? It *abhavat*, became; *sat ca*, the formed (gross); *tyat ca*, and the formless (subtle). The formed and the formless, existing in the Self in their state of unmanifested name and form, are manifested by the indwelling Self; and even when manifested and known as the formed and the formless, they still continue to be inseparable from the Self in time and space. Having this fact in view, it is said that the Self became these two. Moreover, the (Self became) *niruktam ca aniruktam ca*, the definable and the undefinable. *Nirukta* is that which is definable as 'this is that', by distinguishing it from things of its own class as also from things of other classes, and by associating it with a certain time and space. *Anirukta* is its opposite. *Nirukta* and *anirukta*, too, are but attributes of the formed and the formless. Just as the formed and the formless are the visible and invisible, so also are the *nilayanam ca anilayanam ca*, the sustaining and the non-sustaining. *Nilayana* means a nest, that which supports; and this is an attribute of the formed. *Anilayana*, a non-supporting thing—is opposed to that (*nilayana*) and is an attribute of the formless. Though 'invisible', 'undefinable', and 'non-supporting' are the attributes of the formless, they relate only to the manifested state, for they are referred to in the Vedas as occurring after creation. By *tyat*, the formless, are meant the vital force etc. which are inexpressible, and it is non-sustaining as well. So, all these adjectives belonging to the formless, relate to the manifested (created). *Vijñānam* is sentient, and *avijñānam* is devoid of that (sentience), insentient stone etc. It follows from the context that *satyam* is truth falling within the range of the empirical, and not absolute truth. For the absolute truth is only one, which is Brahman. But here the relative truth, as found in the empirical world, is referred to; as for instance, water is said to be true in comparison with the water in a mirage which is false. *Anṛtam*, untruth, is the opposite of that. Again, what is it that *abhavat*, became, all this? That which is *satyam*, the absolute truth. What is that, again? It is Brahman; for it is Brahman that has been introduced as the topic of discussion by the sentence, 'Brahman is truth, knowledge, infinite.' The knowers of Brahman *ācaksate*, call It; *satyam*, truth; because it is the one Brahman, called *satya*, truth, that *abhavat*, became; *yat kim ca idam*, all this that there is—all modifications, without any exception, starting with the visible and the invisible, all of which are the features of the formed and the formless—, there being no existence for any of these modifications of name and form apart from that Brahman.

The question that was mooted after the teacher's instruction concerned existence and non-existence. As an answer to this, it has been said that the Self desired, 'I shall become many.' After creating, in accordance with His wish, such products as space etc. which are characterized as the visible and invisible etc., and then entering into them, He became many through His acts of seeing, hearing, thinking, and knowing. Hence it is implied thereby that this Self must be accepted as existing, since It is the cause of space etc., exists in this creation, is lodged in the supreme space within the cavity of the heart, and is perceived through Its diverse reflections on the mental concepts.[1]

Tat, pertaining to this—concerning this idea expressed in the *brāhmaṇa* portion; *eṣaḥ ślokaḥ bhavati*, occurs this verse. Just as in the preceding five chapters occurred verses expressive of the selves, counting from the one constituted by food, so, too, is there this verse which indicates through Its effects the existence of the Self as the inmost of all.

CHAPTER VII

असद्वा इदमग्र आसीत्। ततो वै सदजायत।
तदात्मानꣳ स्वयमकुरुत। तस्मात्तत्सुकृतमुच्यत इति।

[1] The mental concepts are 'I am a doer', 'I am an enjoyer', etc.; and these, again, being the different appearances of the light of the Self, reveal the Self in Its conditioned form, and not in Its unconditioned essence.

यद्वै तत् सुकृतम्। रसो वै सः। रसꣳ ह्येवायं लब्ध्वाऽऽनन्दी भवति। को ह्येवान्यात्कः प्राण्यात्। यदेष आकाश आनन्दो न स्यात्। एष ह्येवाऽऽनन्दयाति। यदा ह्येवैष एतस्मिन्नदृश्येऽनात्म्येऽनिरुक्तेऽनिलयनेऽभयं प्रतिष्ठां विन्दते। अथ सोऽभयं गतो भवति। यदा ह्येवैष एतस्मिन्नुदरमन्तरं कुरुते। अथ तस्य भयं भवति। तत्त्वेव भयं विदुषोऽमन्वानस्य। तदप्येष श्लोको भवति ॥१॥ इति सप्तमोऽनुवाकः ॥

1. In the beginning all this was but the unmanifested (Brahman). From that emerged the manifested. That Brahman created Itself by Itself. Therefore It is called the self-creator.

That which is known as the self-creator is verily the source of joy; for one becomes happy by coming in contact with that source of joy. Who, indeed, will inhale, and who will exhale, if this Bliss be not there in the supreme space (within the heart). This one, indeed, enlivens (people). For whenever an aspirant gets fearlessly established in this unperceivable, bodiless, inexpressible and unsupporting Brahman, he reaches the state of fearlessness. For, whenever the aspirant creates the slightest difference in It, he is smitten with fear. Nevertheless, that very Brahman is a terror to the (so called) learned man who lacks the unitive outlook.

Illustrative of this here is a verse:

Asat vai idam agre āsīt, in the beginning all this was but the unmanifested (Brahman). By the word *asat* is meant the unmanifested state of Brahman as contrasted with the state in which distinctions of name and form become manifested. Not that absolute non-existence (the root meaning of the word, *asat*) is meant, for the existent cannot come out of the non-existent. *Idam*, this standing for the manifested world possessed of the distinctions of name and form; *agre*, in the beginning—before creation; *āsīt asat*, was but Brahman that could be called *asat*. *Tataḥ*, from that—from that Unmanifested; *vai*, indeed; *sat*, that which is distinguished by manifested name and form; *ajāyata*, was born. Is the effect entirely separate from that (cause), just as a son is from the father? The answer is being given negatively: *Tat*, that which is called the Unmanifested (Brahman); *svayam*, Itself; *akuruta*, created; *ātmānam*, Itself. Since this is so, *tasmāt*, therefore; *tat*, that Brahman Itself; *ucyate*, is called; the *sukṛtam*, self-creator.[1] By virtue of being the cause of everything, Brahman is well recognized in this world as the self-creator. Or, since Brahman Itself created everything by virtue of Its being everything, therefore that very Brahman, which is the cause from the standpoint of virtue as well, is called *sukṛta* (merit).[2] At all events, whether the meaning of *sukṛta* be 'merit' or it be the other one (*self-creator*), that cause which brings (one) into association etc. with a result is familiarly known in the world as *sukṛta*. That well known fact is possible only if there is an eternal consciousness acting as the cause. Hence, from the well known fact of *sukṛta*, it follows that Brahman exists.

[1] *Sukṛtam* (standing for *svakṛta*) should mean 'self-created'. But Śaṅkara takes it as a Vedic licence for 'self-creator'. —Ā.G.

[2] *Sukṛta* (lit. well-done) means merit, which is one of the causes of creation.

It exists because of this further reason. Of which reason? Since It is the source of joy. How is Brahman well known as the source of joy? The answer is: *Yat vai tat sukṛtam*, that which is known as the self-creator; *rasaḥ vai saḥ*, is verily the *rasaḥ*, (a source of joy). *Rasaḥ* stands for anything that is a means for satisfaction, i.e. a source of joy, such as sweet and sour things which are well known to be so in the world. *Rasam labdhvā*, getting a thing of joy; *ayam bhavati*, one becomes; *ānandī*, happy. A nonentity is not seen in this world to be a cause of happiness. Inasmuch as those Brāhmaṇas who have realized Brahman are seen to be as happy as one is from obtaining an external source of joy — though, in fact, they do not take help of any external means of happiness, make no effort, and cherish no desire —, it follows, as a matter of course, that Brahman is, indeed, the source of their joy. Hence there does exist that Brahman which is full of joy[1] and is the spring of their happiness.

Brahman exists because of this additional reason. Of which? Since such actions as exhaling are seen. This body, too, of a living being, exhales through that function of the vital force called *prāṇa* and inhales through that other called *apāna*. Thus are the body and senses, in their association, seen to perform their vital and organic functions. This coming into association for serving a common purpose is not possible unless there

[1] Taking the expression, *rasavat*, to mean 'like a juice, i.e. like a sweet thing' (instead of 'full of joy'), the concluding portion may be translated thus: '. . . Brahman which is the spring of their happiness just as a sweet thing is.'

is a sentient being which is not a part of this conglomeration. For such is not the case anywhere else.[1] That fact is being stated: *yat*, if; *eṣaḥ ānandaḥ*, this Bliss; *na syāt*, should not be there; *ākāśe*, in the (supreme) space that is lodged in the cavity of the heart; then in this world, *kaḥ hi eva*, who, indeed; *anyāt*, would inhale, i.e. perform the function of *apāna*; or *kaḥ prāṇyāt*, who would exhale, i.e. perform the function of *prāṇa*? Therefore that Brahman, for whose purpose there are such activities of the body and senses, as exhaling etc., does exist; and the happiness of people is caused by That itself. How? *Eṣaḥ hi eva*, this one, this supreme Self, indeed; *ānandayāti* (i.e. *ānandayati*), enlivens—people, in accordance with their merit. The idea is this: That very Self, which is Bliss by nature, is thought of as limited and diversified by people because of their ignorance.

That Brahman exists as the cause of fear and fearlessness of the men of ignorance and knowledge (respectively). For fearlessness comes as a result of taking refuge in something that exists, whereas fear cannot cease by resorting to some thing that does not exist. How does Brahman become the cause of fearlessness? The answer is: *Hi*, since; *yadā eva*, at the very time; that *eṣaḥ*, this one—an aspirant; *etasmin*, in this one—in Brahman—. (In Brahman) of what kind? *Adṛśye*: *dṛśya* is anything that is meant to be seen, that is to say, any modification; for a modification is meant to be

[1] Building materials themselves, for instance, do not erect a structure. A house stands here because somebody built it and yet did not form a part of it.

perceived; what is not a *dṛśya* is *adṛśya*, i.e. changeless. In this *adṛśye*, changeless, that which is not an object of cognition. *Anātmye*, in the unembodied. Since It is imperceptible, It is incorporeal. Since It is incorporeal, It is *aniruktam*, inexpressible. Anything possessed of attributes can alone be expressed in words, and anything possessed of attributes is mutable, whereas Brahman is changeless, It being the source of all modifications. Hence, It is inexpressible. That being so, It is *anilayanam*: *nilayana* is a nest, refuge; *anilayana* is the opposite of that; It is without support. The meaning of the sentence is: (When) in that entity which is this changeless, unembodied, inexpressible, unsustaining Brahman, which is distinct from all the attributes of a product, (the aspirant) *vindate*, gets; *pratiṣṭhām*, stability, Self-absorption; *abhayam*, in a fearless way—. The word *abhayam* (fearlessly) is used adverbially (to modify the verb *vindate*, gets); or it has to be changed in gender to *abhayām* (fearless) to qualify the noun (*pratiṣṭhām*, stability) (When the aspirant gets this fearless stability in Brahman) *atha*, then; since he does not see diversity which is the creation of ignorance and the cause of fear, therefore, *saḥ*, he; *abhayam gataḥ bhavati*, becomes established in fearlessness. When he becomes established in his true nature, then he does not see anything else, does not hear anything else, does not know anything else. Someone gets afraid of someone else, but it is not logical that the Self should be afraid of the Self. Hence the Self is the source of fearlessness for the Self. In spite of the existence of the cause of fear, there are Brāhmaṇas to be found who are indeed free of fear from all quarters. This would be unjustifiable if Brahman, the protector from fear were not there. Therefore, from the fact of noticing their fearlessness, it follows that Brahman exists as the source of that intrepidity. When does that aspirant reach fearlessness? When he does not perceive anything else and does not create any *antaram*, difference, in the Self, then he attains fearlessness. This is the idea.

On the contrary, *hi*, since; *yadā*, when, in the state of ignorance; *eṣaḥ*, this one, the ignorant man; sees in the Self something presented by nescience, like the vision of a second moon seen by a man suffering from the eye-disease called *timira*; and *etasmin*, in this, in Brahman; *kurute*, he perceives; *ut aram*, even a slight; *antaram*, hole, difference—since the perception of difference is the cause of fear,[1] it means that even if he sees the slightest difference—; *atha*, then, because of that seeing of difference; *bhayam bhavati*, fear crops up for this soul that perceives difference. So the Self alone is the cause of fear to the self in the case of an ignorant man. The Upaniṣad states that very fact here: *Tu* nevertheless; *tat eva*, that very Brahman; is *bhayam*, a terror; *viduṣaḥ*, to the man of (apparent) learning, who perceives difference; that very Brahman, when perceived through (a sense of) duality and called God, becomes a terror for the (apparently) learned man who knows thus, 'God is different from me, and I am a worldly creature different from God', and who creates the slightest difference. (It becomes a terror) *amanvānasya*, for him who does not view from the stand-

1 Another reading is *bhedadarśanam eva hi antarakaraṇam*—'the seeing of difference itself is the creator of difference'.

point of unity. Accordingly, the man who does not realize the reality that is the Self, which is one and undifferentiated, is surely unenlightened, though he may be learned. Anyone who considers oneself destructible becomes struck with fear at the very sight of a destructive agency. A destroyer (in the ultimate analysis) can be so, only if it is itself indestructible.[1] Now, if there be no cause of destruction, there should be no such fear in the destructible as issues from a perception of a destroyer. The whole world, however, is seen to be stricken with fear. Therefore, from the perceived fact of fear in the world, it follows that there does exist a terrifying thing which is by nature an indestructible agent of destruction, because of which the world shudders.

Expressive of this idea, too, there is this verse:

CHAPTER VIII

भीषाऽस्माद्वातः पवते। भीषोदेति सूर्यः।
भीषाऽस्मादग्निश्चेन्द्रश्च। मृत्युर्धावति पञ्चम इति।

सैषाऽऽनन्दस्य मीमाꣳसा भवति। युवा स्यात्साधुयुवा-ऽध्यायकः। आशिष्ठो दृढिष्ठो बलिष्ठः। तस्येयं पृथिवी सर्वा वित्तस्य पूर्णा स्यात्। स एको मानुष आनन्दः। ते ये शतं मानुषा आनन्दाः ॥१॥ स एको मनुष्यगन्धर्वाणामानन्दः। श्रोत्रियस्य चाकामहतस्य। ते ये शतं मनुष्यगन्धर्वाणा-

[1] The ultimate cause of fear must itself be indestructible, since a contrary supposition will lead to an infinite regress. And such an eternal agent is Brahman.

मानन्दाः। स एको देवगन्धर्वाणामानन्दः। श्रोत्रियस्य चाकामहतस्य। ते ये शतं देवगन्धर्वाणामानन्दाः। स एकः पितृणां चिरलोकलोकानामानन्दः। श्रोत्रियस्य चाकामहतस्य। ते ये शतं पितृणां चिरलोकलोकानामानन्दाः। स एक आजान-जानां देवानामानन्दः ॥२॥ श्रोत्रियस्य चाकामहतस्य। ते ये शतमाजानजानां देवानामानन्दाः। स एकः कर्मदेवानां देवानामानन्दः। ये कर्मणा देवानपियन्ति। श्रोत्रियस्य चाकामहतस्य। ते ये शतं कर्मदेवानां देवानामानन्दाः। स एको देवानामानन्दः। श्रोत्रियस्य चाकामहतस्य। ते ये शतं देवानामानन्दाः। स एक इन्द्रस्याऽऽनन्दः ॥३॥ श्रोत्रि-यस्य चाकामहतस्य। ते ये शतमिन्द्रस्याऽऽनन्दाः। स एको बृहस्पतेरानन्दः। श्रोत्रियस्य चाकामहतस्य। ते ये शतं बृह-स्पतेरानन्दाः। स एकः प्रजापतेरानन्दः। श्रोत्रियस्य चाका-महतस्य। ते ये शतं प्रजापतेरानन्दाः। स एको ब्रह्मण आनन्दः। श्रोत्रियस्य चाकामहतस्य ॥४॥

1–4. Out of His fear the Wind blows. Out of fear the Sun rises. Out of His fear runs Fire, as also Indra, and Death, the fifth.

This, then, is an evaluation of that Bliss:

Suppose there is a young man—in the prime of life, good, learned, most expeditious, most strongly built, and most energetic. Suppose there lies this earth for him filled with wealth. This will be one unit of human joy.[1] If this human joy be multiplied a hundred times, it is one joy of the man-Gandharvas, and so also of a follower of the Vedas unaffected by desires. If this joy

[1] A unit of measurement for the estimation of Bliss.

of the man-Gandharvas be multiplied a hundred times, it is one joy of the divine-Gandharvas, and so also of a follower of the Vedas unaffected by desire. If the joy of the divine-Gandharvas be increased a hundredfold, it is one joy of the manes whose world is everlasting, and so of a follower of the Vedas untouched by desire. If the joy of the manes that dwell in the everlasting world be increased a hundredfold, it is one joy of those that are born as gods in heaven, and so of a follower of the Vedas untouched by desire. If the joy of those that are born as gods in heaven be multiplied a hundredfold, it is one joy of the gods called the Karma-Devas, who reach the gods through Vedic rites, and so of a follower of the Vedas unaffected by desire. If the joy of the gods, called the Karma-Devas, be multiplied a hundredfold, it is one joy of the gods, and so of a follower of the Vedas untarnished by desire. If the joy of the gods be increased a hundred times, it is one joy of Indra, and so of a follower of the Vedas untouched by desire. If the joy of Indra be multiplied a hundredfold, it is one joy of Bṛhaspati, and so of a follower of the Vedas unaffected by desire. If the joy of Bṛhaspati be increased a hundred times, it is one joy of Virāṭ, and so of a follower of the Vedas untarnished by desire. If the joy of Virāṭ be multiplied a hundred times, it is one joy of Hiraṇyagarbha, and so is it of the follower of the Vedas unsullied by desire.

Bhīṣā, through fear; *asmāt*, of Him; *vātaḥ pavate*, (the god of) Wind blows. *Bhīṣā*, through fear; *udeti*, rises; *sūryaḥ*, the Sun. *Bhīṣā asmāt*, through fear of Him; *dhāvati*, runs; *agniḥ ca indraḥ ca*, Fire as also Indra; (and) *mṛtyuḥ pañcamaḥ*, Death, the fifth. Since Wind etc., greatly adorable and lordly though they themselves are, engage regularly in such highly strenuous works as blowing, it is reasonable to conclude that this is possible on the supposition of a ruler different from them, because of whom they have their disciplined activity. Since they engage (in their duties) out of fear of this Brahman, just as servants do out of fear of a king, therefore, Brahman does exist as their ruler as a terrifying entity.

And that Brahman, the source of fear, is Bliss. *Eṣā bhavati*, this is; *mīmāṁsā*, an evaluation; *ānandasya*, of Bliss, of the aforesaid Brahman. What is there to be assessed about Bliss? The answer is: Bliss can be studied thus from this point of view—whether It arises from the contact of subject and object, as is the case with worldly happiness, or whether It is natural. As to that, the worldly bliss attains excellence owing to a concurrence of external and internal means. The bliss, thus attained, is being instanced here as an approach to the Bliss that is Brahman; for through this familiar bliss can be approached the Bliss that is comprehensible by an intellect free from objective thought. Even worldly bliss is a particle of the Bliss that is Brahman, which becomes transmuted into impermanent worldly bliss, consequent on knowledge becoming covered up by ignorance, and ignorance becoming successively thicker according as the individuals, starting with Hiraṇyagarbha, think diversely of this Bliss under the impulsion of the result of their past actions and in conformity with their past contemplations, and under the influence of contact with accessories like objects etc. That very Bliss which is visualized by one who is learned, versed in the Vedas and free from passion, appears diversely as increasing more and more—a hundredfold each time in the planes starting with that of man-Gandharvas till the bliss of Hiraṇyagarbha, Brahmā, is reached—, in accordance with the attenuation of ignorance, desire and action. But when the division of subject and object, created by ignorance is eliminated by enlightenment, there is only the intrinsic all pervading Bliss that is one without a second. In order to impart this idea, the text says: *yuvā syāt*, etc.

Yuvā, a youth—one in the prime of life. *Sādhu-yuvā* is an adjective of the youth, and means one who is both young and good. Even a youth may be bad, and even a good man may not be young. Hence the specification, 'Suppose there is a young man who is a good youth.' *Adhyāyakaḥ* is one who has studied the Vedas. *Āśiṣṭhaḥ*, the best ruler (or, 'the quickest in action').[1] *Dṛḍhiṣṭhaḥ*, most hardy (i.e. having all the senses intact). *Baliṣṭhaḥ*, strongest. (Suppose the youth is) blessed with such physical accessories. (And let there be) *tasya*, for him; *iyam sarvā pṛthivī*, this whole earth; *pūrṇā*, filled; *vittasya*, (should rather be *vittena*), with wealth meant for enjoyment, and with the means of *karmas* leading to seen and unseen results. The idea is that he is a king ruling over the earth. *Saḥ*, the joy that he has; is *ekaḥ mānuṣaḥ ānandaḥ*, a single human bliss, one unit of the highest human bliss. *Te ye śatam mānuṣāḥ ānandāḥ*, that human bliss multiplied a hundredfold; is *saḥ ekaḥ manuṣya-gandharvāṇām ānandaḥ*, one unit of the bliss of the man-Gandharvas. The happiness of man-Gandharvas becomes a hundred times better

[1] See Ś.

than that of man. Man-Gandharvas are those human beings who become Gandharvas through some special *karmas* and meditations. As they are possessed of the power of disappearance etc., being endowed with subtle bodies and senses, so obstacles in their way are few, and they are endowed with the power and means of resisting dualities (such as heat and cold, etc.). Therefore, a man-Gandharva will have mental tranquillity inasmuch as he remains unopposed and can withstand duality. From that excellence of tranquillity follows an abundant expression of Bliss. Thus it stands to reason that in proportion to the abundance of tranquillity on the succeeding planes as compared with that on the preceding ones, the excellence of bliss also progresses a hundredfold. However, the man free from desire has not been taken into consideration at the initial stage with a view to showing that the bliss of one, who observes Vedic duties and is untouched by desire and enjoyment of human objects, is a hundred times higher than the human bliss and is comparable to that of a man-Gandharva. Devotion to Vedic duties and sinlessness (Bṛ. IV. iii. 33) are implied by the two terms 'learned' and 'young and good'. These two qualities are, indeed, common to all (the planes). But desirelessness has been treated distinctively in order to point out that increase of bliss is independent of the superiority or inferiority of objects. Thus since happiness is seen to improve a hundredfold proportionately with the advance of desirelessness, it is treated here with a view to enjoining dispassionateness as a means for the attainment of supreme Bliss. The rest has been already explained.

Deva-Gandharvāḥ, the divine-Gandharvas, are so from their very birth. The term *ciralokalokānām*, of those whose world lasts for ever, is an adjective of *pitṛṇām*, of the manes, the manes being so qualified since their world lasts (relatively) for ever. *Ājāna* is the world of the gods; those who are born there—born in the regions of gods as a result of special rites prescribed by the *Smṛtis*—are the *Ājānaja* gods. The *karmadevāḥ* are those who reach the gods by mere Vedic Karma, such as Agnihotra etc. The *devāḥ*, gods, are those who are thirtythree in number[1] and receive oblations. Indra is their lord. His preceptor is Bṛhaspati. Prajāpati is Virāṭ who has the three worlds (earth, heaven, and intermediate space) as his body.[2] Brahmā pervades the whole universe in the form of the cosmic and individual persons. This Brahmā is Hiraṇyagarbha in whom all these varieties of bliss become unified, and in whom resides virtue which is the cause of that bliss, consciousness of that bliss, and dispassionateness of the highest order. This bliss of His is directly experienced everywhere by one who is versed in the Vedas, free from sin and unsullied by desire. Hence it is understood that these three qualities are the means (for the attainment of Bliss). Of these, Vedic learning and sinlessness are invariable (in all the planes), whereas desirelessness increases; and hence the last is known to be the best means. The bliss of Brahmā, experienced on the perfection of desirelessness and also open to the direct vision of one who follows the Vedas, is a particle or bit

[1] Eight Vasus, eleven Rudras, twelve Ādityas, Indra, and Prajāpati.

[2] See Commentary on Bṛ. III. iii. 2.

of the supreme Bliss, in accordance with the Vedic text, 'On a particle of this very Bliss other beings live' (Bṛ. IV. iii. 32). This bliss (of Brahmā and others) is a particle of that Supreme Bliss that is natural, from which it has separated like spray from the sea and into which it merges again. In It (the Supreme Bliss) there is no bifurcation of the joy and the enjoyer, since It is non-dual.

The result of this evaluation is being concluded here:

स यश्चायं पुरुषे। यश्चासावादित्ये। स एकः। स य एवंवित्। अस्माल्लोकात्प्रेत्य। एतमन्नमयमात्मानमुपसंक्रामति। एतं प्राणमयमात्मानमुपसंक्रामति। एतं मनोमयमात्मानमुपसंक्रामति। एतं विज्ञानमयमात्मानमुपसंक्रामति। एतमानन्दमयमात्मानमुपसंक्रामति। तदप्येष श्लोको भवति ॥५॥ इति अष्टमोऽनुवाकः ॥

5. He that is here in the human person, and He that is there in the sun, are one. He who knows thus attains, after desisting from this world, this self made of food, attains this self made of the vital force, attains this self made of mind, attains this self made of intelligence, attains this self made of bliss.

Expressive of this there occurs this verse:

He who, after projecting all the creation—beginning with space and ending with the body made of (the essence of) food entered into it and is lodged in the supreme space within the cavity of the heart, is here indicated by the words *saḥ yaḥ*, He who. Who is He?

Ayam puruṣe yaḥ ca asau āditye, He who is in the human person, and He who resides in the sun. The supreme Bliss, that has been indicated as directly perceptible to the follower of the Vedas, and on a particle of which subsist all the beings worthy of joy—counting from Brahmā—, that supreme Bliss is being described as 'He who resides in the sun'. He is one in the same sense that the space in a pot, standing separately, is one with space (as such).

Objection: In the matter of describing that Bliss, the corporeal soul should not be referred to in general terms by saying, 'He that is in the human person'; rather it is proper to indicate that soul by saying, 'And He that is in the right eye' (Bṛ. II.iii.5, IV.ii.2, V.v.2.), that being better known.

Answer: No, for the discussion is here about the supreme Self.[1] The supreme Self certainly forms the subject matter here in the texts, 'In the unperceivable, bodiless' (II.vii), 'Out of His fear the Wind blows' (II. viii. 1), 'This, then, is an evaluation of that Bliss' (*ibid*). It is not reasonable to refer suddenly to something out of context. And the subject sought to be taught is the knowledge of the supreme Self.[2] There-

[1] The other text quoted above refers to a meditation based on the identity of the individual soul and Hiraṇyagarbha, and not to the identity, as such, of the individual Self and the supreme Self.

[2] 'The same unsurpassing Bliss of the conscious Reality that is reflected on a superior medium, viz the sun, is also reflected on an inferior medium, viz a human being possessing head, hands, etc. Thus, from the standpoint of supreme Bliss, the two distinct entities are on a par, and intrinsically they are the same. This is what is taught.' —Ā.G.

fore, it is verily the supreme Self that is referred to in the expression, *saḥ ekaḥ*, He is one.

Objection: Is not the topic started with an estimation of Bliss? The result of that estimation, too, has to be concluded by saying: 'The Bliss that is non-different and intrinsic, and not a product of the contact between the subject and the object, is the supreme Self.'

Counter-objection: Is not this indication (of the Self) by eliminating the distinctions pertaining to the different loci, — which we come across here in the sentence, 'He that is here in the human person, and He that is there in the sun, are one' —, quite in line with that?

Objection: Even so, is it not useless to single out the sun?

Answer: No, it is not useless, because it is meant for obviating (notions of) superiority and inferiority. In the sun is found the highest perfection of duality, consisting of the formed and the formless. If, from the standpoint of the supreme Bliss, that perfection can be placed on the same footing with the human personality, after eliminating the peculiarities of the latter, there will remain no superiority or inferiority for one who attains that goal; and hence it becomes reasonable to say that 'he reaches a state of fearlessness' (II.vii).

The question as to whether Brahman exists or not, raised after the teacher's instruction, has been dealt with. One of these post-questions has been dismissed by saying that from the reasonings which justify the phenomena of creation, acquisition of joy, functioning of life, reaching a state of fearlessness, and experience of fear, it follows that Brahman does exist as the cause of those space etc. There are two other post-questions relating to the attainment or non-attainment of Brahman by the enlightened man and the unenlightened man. Of these, the last post-question is, 'Does the enlightened man attain or does he not?' In order to settle this, it is being said (as below). The middle post-question is settled by the answer to the last one; and hence no (separate) effort is made for solving it.

Saḥ yaḥ, anyone who; is *evamvit*, a knower of this kind; who, having discarded all ideas of superiority and inferiority, knows Brahman, described earlier, *evam*, in this manner, 'I am the non-dual truth, knowledge, infinity';—for the word, '*evam*, thus', is used for alluding to some topic already mooted—; what does he become?—he, *pretya*, (lit. after departing), desisting, without expecting anything; *asmāt lokāt*, from this world—the totality of things seen and unseen is verily indicated by the term 'this world'; without expecting anything from that world—; *upasaṁkrāmati*, attains; *etam annamayam ātmānam*, this body built up by food, as explained already. The idea is that he does not perceive the totality of objects as different from the self, i.e. the body, built up by food; he sees all the gross elements as identical with the self built up by food.[1] Then he attains *etam prāṇamayam ātmānam*, this body constituted by the vital force, which is itself undivided and is inside the (cosmic) body built up by all the food. Then he attains this body made of mind, the body made of in-

[1] He attains identity with Virāt, the gross Cosmic Person, whose body is constituted by the three worlds—earth, heaven, and intermediate space.

telligence,[1] the body made of bliss. Then he reaches the state of fearlessness in the unperceivable, bodiless, inexpressible, and unsupporting (Self) (II.vii).

With regard to that, this has got to be considered: What is he who knows thus, and how does he attain? Is the attainer different from or the same as the supreme Self? What follows from that? Should the attainer be different, the conclusion will run counter to such Vedic texts as 'Having created that, He entered into that very thing' (II.vi), '(One who worships another god thinking), "He is one, I am another", he does not know' (Bṛ. I.iv.10), 'One only, without a second' (Ch. VI.ii.1), and 'Thou art that' (Ch. VI.viii–xvi). On the contary, if the Self Itself attains the blissful self, we shall be faced with the unsoundness of the same entity being both subject and object; moreover, the supreme Self will either be reduced to a transmigratory soul or a nonentity.

Objection: The discussion is useless if the fault that arises on either assumption be unavoidable. On the other hand, if either of the assumptions is free from defect, or if a third flawless assumption is so, then that alone is the meaning of the scripture, and hence that the discussion is uncalled for.

Answer: No, for the discussion is meant for its ascertainment. True it is that the accruing defect cannot be avoided by accepting either of the two positions, and

[1] Hiraṇyagarbha, conceived of as possessing the powers of action, will, and knowledge, has a subtle body constituted by the totality of vital, mental, and intellectual energy.

that the discussion becomes useless if a third flawless position is ascertained; but that third alternative has not been determined. Hence this consideration is fruitful as it is calculated to lead to that ascertainment.

Objection: True it is that an investigation is fruitful so far as it culminates in the fixing of the meaning of a scripture. But in your case, you will simply cogitate without ever hitting upon any meaning.

Answer: Is it your view that there can occur any Vedic sentence whose meaning need not be determined?

Objection: No.

Counter-objection: How then (is the discussion useless)?

Objection: Because there are many opponents. You are a monist, since you follow the Vedic ideas, while the dualists are many who are outside the Vedic pale and who are opposed to you. Therefore I apprehend that you will not be able to determine.

Answer: This itself is a blessing for me that you brand me as sworn to monism and faced by many who are wedded to plurality. Therefore I shall conquer all; and so I begin the discussion.

The attainer must be the supreme Self alone, inasmuch as merger into that state is the idea implied. What is sought to be imparted here in the text, 'The knower of Brahman attains the highest' (II.i), is becoming the supreme Self through Its knowledge. Surely, it is not possible that one thing can become something else.

Objection: Is it not also unsound to say that the individual soul becomes the supreme Self?

Answer: No, for the idea conveyed is that of removal

of the identity (with the body etc.) created by ignorance. The attainment of one's own Self through the knowledge of Brahman, that is taught, is meant for the elimination of the distinct selves—such as the food-self, the products of nescience—which are really non-Selves, superimposed as Selves.

Objection: How is such a meaning understood?

Answer: Because knowledge alone is prescribed. The effect of knowledge is seen to be the eradication of ignorance; and here that knowledge alone is prescribed as the means for the attainment of the Self.

Objection: May not that be like the communicating of information about a path? So the mere prescription of knowledge as a means does not amount to showing that the supreme Self is the Self of the attainer.

Counter-objection: Why?

Opponent: For it is seen that, in the matter of reaching a different place, the information about the way is communicated. Not that the village itself can be the goer.[1]

Answer: Not so, for the analogy is inept.[2] In the illustration cited, the information imparted is not of the village, but the knowledge imparted there is only of the path, leading to one's arrival there. But in this

[1] The traveller is not the village, though the knowledge of the path to the village is valuable to him. Similarly, the individual is not Brahman, though the instruction about knowledge of Brahman is valuable; for by practising it he can reach Brahman.

[2] One does not say, 'You are the village', when talking about the path leading to it, whereas the identity of the two is taught here explicitly.

case, no information about any other means apart from the knowledge of Brahman is imparted.

Objection: The knowledge of Brahman, as depending on such means as rites etc. enjoined earlier, is taught as a means for the attainment of the highest.

Answer: No, for this was refuted earlier by saying, 'Since liberation is eternal,' etc.[1] And the text, 'Having created that, He entered into that very thing' (II.vi), shows that the Self, immanent in creation, is identical with That (Supreme Brahman). And this follows also from the logic of attaining the state of fearlessness. For if the man of enlightenment sees nothing as different from his own Self, then the statement, 'He gets established in that state of fearlessness', becomes appropriate, since (for him) nothing exists as a separate entity which can cause fear. Moreover, if duality is a creation of nescience, then only is the realization of its insubstantiality through knowledge reasonable; for (the proof of) the non-existence of a second moon consists in its not being seen by one whose eyes are not affected by the disease called *timira*.

Objection: But non-perception of duality is not thus a matter of experience.

Answer: No, for duality is not perceived by a person who is deeply asleep or absorbed in the Self.

Objection: The non-perception of duality in deep sleep is comparable to the non-perception by one who is preoccupied with something else.

Answer: Not so, for then (i.e. in sleep and *samādhi*)

[1] Brahman is identical with liberation, and as such, It is not to be attained. But we can know Brahman in the sense that our ignorance about It is removed.

there is non-perception of everything (so that there can be no preoccupation with anything).

Objection: Duality has existence because of its perception in the dream and waking states.

Answer: No, for the dream and waking states are creations of ignorance. The perception of duality that occurs in the dream and waking states is the result of ignorance, because it ceases on the cessation of ignorance.

Objection: The non-perception (of duality) in sleep is also a result of ignorance.

Answer: No, for it is intrinsic. The reality of a substance consists in its not being mutable, for it does not depend on anything else. Mutability is not a reality, since that depends on other factors. The reality of a substance surely cannot be dependent on external agencies. Any peculiarity that arises in an existing substance is a result of external agencies, and a peculiarity implies change. The perceptions occurring in the dream and waking states are but modal expressions, for the reality of a thing is that which exists in its own right, and the unreality is that which depends on others, inasmuch as it ceases with the cessation of others. Hence, unlike what happens in the dream and waking states, no modality occurs in deep sleep, for the non-perception in the latter state is natural.

For those, however, for whom God is different from the self, and creation, too, is distinct, there is no elimination of fear, since fear is caused by something different. And, something different that is true, cannot have its reality annihilated, nor can a non-existent emerge into being.

Objection: Something external becomes the source of fear when it is supplemented by others.[1]

Answer: No, for that, too, stands on an equal footing. Because, that permanent or impermanent agency[2], in the form of demerit etc., depending on which that something else (i.e. God) becomes the cause of fear for others, cannot have self-effacement by the very fact of what that agency (*adṛṣṭa*) is assumed to be;[3] or should that have self extinction, the real and the unreal will become mutually convertible, so that nobody will have any faith in anything. From the standpoint of non-duality, however, that objection has no bearing, since the world along with its cause is a superimposition through ignorance. For a second moon, seen by a man afflicted by the eye-disease called *timira*, does not attain any reality, nor is it annihilated.

Objection: Knowledge and ignorance are qualities of the Self.[4]

Answer: Not so, for they are perceived. Discrimination (i.e. knowledge) and non-discrimination (i.e.

[1] God, in association with merits and demerits of creatures, causes fear. But the liberated man has no fear of God since he is independent of merit etc.

[2] *Adṛṣṭa*, unseen future result, whose help God takes.

[3] This above view cannot be advanced either by the Sāṁkhyas or the Naiyāyikas; for the former do not believe that an existing demerit can be wholly annihilated; and the latter do not say that so long as demerit persists, its effect will be totally absent. *Adṛṣṭa* also creates the same difficulty.

[4] If knowledge removes ignorance, then both of them must be qualities of the soul, and the soul must be subject to mutation by their emergence or disappearance.

ignorance) are directly perceived, like colour etc., as existing in the mind. Not that colour, perceived as an object, can be an attribute of the perceiver. And ignorance is ascertained by such forms of its perception as, 'I am ignorant', 'My knowledge is indistinct'. Similarly, the distinction of knowledge (from the Self) is perceived, and the enlightened people communicate the knowledge of the Self to others; and so, too, do others grasp it. Accordingly, knowledge and ignorance are to be ranked with name and form; and name and form are not attributes of the Self,[1] in accordance with another Vedic text, '(That which is indeed called Space) is the manifester of name and form. That in which they two exist is Brahman' (Ch. VIII.xiv.1). And those name and form are imagined to exist in Brahman like night and day in the sun, though in reality they are not there.

Objection: If (the Self and Brahman are) non-different, then there arises the absurdity of the same entity becoming the subject and object, as mentioned in the text, 'He attains this self made of bliss' (II. viii 5).

Answer: Not so, for the attainment consists in mere enlightenment. The reaching taught here is no like

[1] 'The beginningless and inscrutable nescience, dependent on pure Consciousness for its existence, gets transformed as the internal organ. That organ, again, gets modified in the form of real knowledge and error in accordance with the preponderance of its *sāttvika* or *tāmasika* qualities. The substance called Consciousness, when reflected on such an organ, is either called enlightened or deluded. In reality Consciousness is neither enlightened nor unelightened.' —Ā.G.

that by a leech. How then? The text treating of attainment means merely realization.[1]

Objection: Attainment in the literal sense is meant here by the expression *upasaṁkrāmati*.

Answer: Not so, for this is not seen in the case of the body made of food; for in the case one reaching the (cosmic) food-body (i.e. Virāt), one is not seen to reach out from this external world like a leech or in any other manner.

Objection: (Attainment is possible in the sense that) the mental body or the intellectual body, when it has gone out (in dream etc.), can return to acquire its own natural state again.

Answer: No, for there can be no action on one's own Self. (Moreover), the topic raised (by you) was that somebody, different from the food-body reaches the food-body; to say now that either the mental body or the intellectual body reaches its own state involves a contradiction. Similarly, the reaching its own state by the blissful-self is not possible.[2]

Therefore, *saṁkramaṇa* does not mean acquisition, nor does it mean 'reaching' by anyone of them begin-

[1] 'The blissful self is not the supreme Self, nor is there any *saṁkramaṇa* in the sense of entry. But what is meant here is the transcendence or negation of the blissful self, accepted falsely as the Self, through the realizaion of Brahman—not as an object, but as identical with the Self.'—Ā.G.

[2] The opponent might say that the *saṁkramaṇa*, in the case of the blissful self, means the attainment of its natural composure after a sorrowful experience. But this also is open to the objection that this runs counter to the opponent's line of argument, and the existence in one's own nature is not an attainment in the real sense.

ning with the food-body. As a last resort, *saṁkramaṇa* can reasonably consist only in the realization by some entity, other than the selves beginning with the food-self and ending with the blissful-self. If *saṁkramaṇa* means realization alone, then through that *saṁkramaṇa*, i.e. through the rise of knowledge about the difference of the Self (from the non-Self), is removed from that all-pervasive Self—which verily resides within the blissful-self and has entered into creation after projecting all things counting from space to food—the error of thinking of the non-Selves such as the food-body as Itself, which (error) arises from Its association with the cavity of the heart. The word *saṁkramaṇa* is used figuratively with regard to this eradication of error created by ignorance, for in no other way can the attainment of the all-pervading Self be justified. Moreover, there is no other thing (that can reach the Self). Besides, the attainment cannot be of oneself; for a leech does not reach itself. Hence, it is with a view to realizing the Self, which has been defined above in the text, 'Brahman is truth, knowledge, infinity' (II.i), that becoming many, entering into creation, acquisition of bliss, fearlessness, attainment, etc. have been attributed to Brahman conceived of as the basis of all empirical dealings; but with regard to the really transcendental Brahman, beyond all conditions, there can be no such ascription.

Tat api, with regard to this also—with regard to the fact that by reaching, i.e. realizing, the unconditioned Self by stages in this way, one ceases to have any fear from anywhere, and one gets established in the state that is fearlessness—; *eṣaḥ ślokaḥ bhavati*, there occurs this verse. This verse stands for expressing briefly the meaning of the whole topic, the gist of this Part called the *Ānandavallī*, the Part *On Bliss*.

CHAPTER IX

यतो वाचो निवर्तन्ते। अप्राप्य मनसा सह।
आनन्दं ब्रह्मणो विद्वान्। न बिभेति कुतश्चनेति।
एतꣳ ह वाव न तपति। किमहꣳ साधु नाकरवम्।
किमहं पापमकरवमिति। स य एवं विद्वानेते आत्मानꣳ
स्पृणुते। उभे ह्येवैष एते आत्मानꣳ स्पृणुते। य एवं वेद।
इत्युपनिषत्॥१॥ इति नवमोऽनुवाकः॥
इति ब्रह्मानन्दवल्ली समाप्ता॥

1. The enlightened man is not afraid of anything after realizing that Bliss of Brahman,[1] failing to reach which, words turn back along with the mind.

Him, indeed, this remorse does not afflict: 'Why did I not perform good deeds, and why did I perform bad deeds?' He who is thus enlightened strengthens the Self with which these two are identical; for it is he, indeed, who knows thus, that can strengthen the Self which these two really are. This is the secret teaching.

Yataḥ, that from which—from the Self, which is

[1] Brahman and *ānanda* (Bliss) are non-different. To speak of Brahman's *ānanda* is like talking of 'the body of a mortar'.—Ś

unconditioned, has the aforesaid definition, and is non-dual and Bliss; *vācaḥ*, words that stand for conditioned objects, (turn back). Though words are applied by their users even with regard to the unconditioned and non-dual Brahman, expecting to express It by taking for granted Its parity with other substances, still those words *aprāpya*, without reaching, without expressing (that Brahman); *nivartante*, turn back, become despoiled of their power. The word *manaḥ* stands for a notion, a cognition. And as a word proceeds to anything, supersensuous though it be, conceptual knowledge also strives to encompass that thing for expressing it as well; and words, too, become active where there is knowledge. Hence words and ideas, speech and mind, move together everywhere. Therefore, that Brahman which is beyond all concepts and all words, and which has such attributes as invisibility, from which words, though used by their utterers in all possible ways for expressing Brahman, return *manasā saha*, together with the mind—with conceptual knowledge that is able to express everything (else); the *vidvān*, one who has known, through the aforesaid process; the *brahmaṇaḥ ānandam*, Bliss of that Brahman—the supreme Bliss of Brahman that is the Self of the follower of the Vedas, who is sinless, unaffected by desire, and wholly free from all craving—, the Bliss that is free from the relation of subject and object, is natural, eternal, and indivisible; (the man of knowledge) having known that Bliss, *na bibheti kutaścana*, is not afraid of anything, for there remains no cause of fear. There certainly does not exist anything, distinct from that man of knowledge, of which he can be afraid; for it has been said that, when anyone creates the slightest difference (in this Brahman) through ignorance, then one is subject to fear (II.vii). But since for the enlightened man the cause of fear, which is the effect of ignorance, has been removed like the second moon seen by a man with diseased eyes, it is proper that he has no fear of anything. This verse was quoted in the context of the mental self as well, because the mind is an aid to the knowledge of Brahman. But there the idea of Brahman was superimposed on the mental self, and then by saying by way of eulogy of that imaginary Brahman that 'one is not subject to fear *at any time*' (II.iv), fear alone was denied; but by saying, 'he is not *afraid of anything*', in the (present) context of the nondual (Brahman), the cause itself of fear is negated,

Objection: But causes of fear, viz omission of good deeds and commission of bad deeds, do persist (even in his case).

Answer: Not so.

Objection: How?

The *answer* is: (Such omission and commission) *na tapati*, do not worry or afflict; *etam*, such a man, who is a knower as aforesaid. *Ha* and *vāva* are particles implying emphasis.

Objection: How, again, omission of virtue and commission of sin do not afflict (him)?

The *answer* is: When death approaches, remorse comes in the form—'*Kim*, why; *na akaravam*, did I not perform; *sādhu*, good deeds?' Similarly, repentance in the form—'*Kim*, why; *akaravam*, I did; *pāpam*, prohibited things?'—comes to him from fear of affliction in the form of falling into hell etc. These two — omission of the good and commission of the bad — do not torment this one, as they do the ignorant man.

Objection: Why, again, do they not afflict the enlightened man?

The *answer* is: *Saḥ yaḥ evam vidvān*, he who knows (Brahman) thus; *spṛṇute*, delights or strengthens; *ete ātmānam*, these two — virtue and vice, the causes of grief — which are (really) the Self. The idea is that he considers both as identified with the supreme Self, *Hi*, since, he who, having divested both virtue and vice of their individual distinctions; has known *ete ātmānam eva*, these two as verily the Self; he *ātmānam spṛṇute*, strengthens the Self. Who? *Yaḥ evam veda*, he that knows Brahman thus — as non-dual and Bliss as described earlier. Virtue and vice, seen by him as identified with the Self, become powerless and harmless, and they do not bring about rebirth. *Iti upaniṣat*, this is the secret instruction — this is the knowledge of Brahman, called *upaniṣad*, which has been stated thus in this Part. The idea is that the most secret of all knowledge has been revealed; for in it is ingrained the highest consummation.

ॐ सह नाववतु। सह नौ भुनक्तु। सह वीर्यं करवावहै।
तेजस्वि नावधीतमस्तु मा विद्विषावहै।

ॐ शान्तिः शान्तिः शान्तिः ॥

PART III

On Bhṛgu's Enlightenment

CHAPTER I

ॐ सह नाववतु। सह नौ भुनक्तु। सह वीर्यं करवा-
वहै। तेजस्वि नावधीतमस्तु मा विद्विषावहै।

ॐ शान्तिः शान्तिः शान्तिः ।।

Since Brahman, that is truth, knowledge, and infinity, brought about this creation—starting with space and ending with the body made of food—, then It entered into it, and seems to be possessed of distinctions because of this fact of entry, therefore one should realize thus: 'I am that very Brahman which is the Bliss that is distinct from all creation and is possessed of such characteristics as invisibility.' For the (subject of) entry (of Brahman) is meant to imply this. In the case of one who knows thus, good and bad deeds do not bring about rebirth. This was the idea intended to be conveyed in the Part *On Bliss* (*Ānanda-vallī*). The knowledge of Brahman, too, has been concluded. After this is to be taught concentration which is helpful to the knowledge of Brahman, as also such meditations with regard to food etc. which have not been dealt with so far. Therefore this Part begins. The story is meant to eulogize knowledge by showing that it was imparted[1] to a dear son by a father.

भृगुर्वै वारुणिः। वरुणं पितरमुपससार। अधीहि भगवो ब्रह्मेति। तस्मा एतत्प्रोवाच। अन्नं प्राणं चक्षुः श्रोत्रं मनो वाचमिति। तꣳ होवाच। यतो वा इमानि भूतानि जायन्ते। येन जातानि जीवन्ति। यत्प्रयन्त्यभिसंविशन्ति। तद्विजिज्ञासस्व। तद् ब्रह्मेति। स तपोऽतप्यत। स तपस्तप्त्वा ॥१॥
इति प्रथमोऽनुवाकः ॥

1. Bhṛgu, the well-known son of Varuṇa, approached his father Varuṇa with the (formal) request, 'O revered sir, teach me Brahman.' To him he (Varuṇa) said this: 'Food, vital force, eye, ear, mind, speech — these are the aids to the knowledge of Brahman).' To him he (Varuṇa) said: 'Crave to know well that from which all these beings take birth, that by which they live after being born, that towards which they move and into which they merge. That is Brahman.' He practised concentration.[2] He, having practised concentration —.

The particle *vai*, alluding to a recognised fact, calls up to memory one who is well known by the name Bhṛgu. *Vāruṇiḥ* is the son of Varuṇa. Varuṇa's son, becoming anxious to know Brahman, *upasasāra*, approached; his *pitaram varuṇam*, father Varuṇa; with,

[1] As a valuable heritage out of affection.

[2] He contemplated with concentration.

iti, this sacred formula (*mantra*): '*Adhīhi bhagavaḥ brahma*, teach (me) Brahman, O revered sir.' *Adhīhi* means teach, tell. And *tasmai*, to him, who had approached in due form; the father, too, *provāca*, spoke; *etat*, this—this sentence: '*Annam*,' etc. He spoke of *annam*, food, i.e. the body; of *prāṇam*, the vital force, which is within that body and which is the eater; and of the aids to cognition, viz *cakṣuḥ*, *śrotram*, *manaḥ*, *vācam*, eye, ear, mind, speech; he spoke of these as the doors to the realization of Brahman.[1] And having spoken of food etc. as doors, he *uvāca*, told; the definition of Brahman, *tam*, to him, Bhṛgu. What is that (definition)? *Yataḥ vai*, that from which, indeed; *imāni bhūtāni*, all these beings—starting with Brahmā and ending with a clump of grass; *jāyante*, take birth; *jātāni*, being born; *yena jīvanti*, that by which they live, grow; *yat*, that Brahman towards which; *prayanti*, they proceed; into which they *abhisaṁviśanti*, enter, become fully identified, at the time of their dissolution—that with which the beings do not lose their identity during the times of creation, existence, and dissolution. This, then, is the definition of Brahman. *Vijijñāsasva*, crave to know well; *tat*, that; *brahma*, Brahman. Realize, through the help of food etc., that Brahman which is defined thus—this is the idea. Another Vedic text, too, shows that these are doors to the realization of Brahman: 'Those who have known the Vital Force of the vital

[1] 'These are *doors* in the sense that they are helpful in distinguishing the object aimed at. For it is from the fact of the impossibility of the activities of the body etc. continuing in any other way (than through the consciousness of the Self) that consciousness becomes distinguished from them as a separate entity.'—Ā.G.

force, the Eye of the eye, the Ear of the ear, the Food of the food, and the Mind of the mind, have realized the ancient, primordial Brahman' (Bṛ. IV. iv. 18). Having heard from his father the doors to the realization of Brahman, as also the definition of Brahman, *saḥ* he, Bhṛgu; *atapyata*, practised; *tapaḥ*, (lit. austerity), concentration—as a means to the realization of Brahman.

Objection: How could Bhṛgu, again, accept *tapaḥ* (concentration) as a means, since it was not taught to be so?

Answer: (He accepted this) because of the incompleteness of the instruction. Varuṇa said that food etc. are the doors to the realization of Brahman, and that Its definition is, 'That from which all these beings take birth,' etc. That, indeed, is incomplete; for Brahman was not directly pointed out there. Otherwise, Brahman, in Its true nature, should have been indicated by saying, 'This Brahman is of this kind', to the son who was desirous of knowing. Not that he indicated thus. How did he do then? He said in an incomplete manner. So it is to be understood that for the knowledge of Brahman the father certainly had some other discipline in view. As for singling out *tapaḥ* (concentration), this is because it is the best discipline, for it is well known in the world that of all the means that are causally related with definite ends, concentration is the best.[1] So Bhṛgu accepted *tapaḥ* as a means to the knowl-

[1] From the father's description of Brahman, Bhṛgu could not arrive at any non-composite, unitary conception of Brahman which ruled out all duality and which could not be analysed back into its component parts; for the description itself was soaked in plurality. Bhṛgu aimed at an irresolvable concept, and hence he

edge of Brahman though it was not taught by his father. This *tapaḥ* consists in the concentration of the outer and inner organs, for that forms the door to the knowledge of Brahman in accordance with the Smṛti, 'The concentration of the mind and the senses is the highest *tapaḥ*. Since it is higher than all the virtues, it is called the highest virtue' (Mbh. Śā. 250.4).

And *saḥ*, he; *tapaḥ taptvā*, having practised concentration—.

CHAPTER II

अन्नं ब्रह्मेति व्यजानात्। अन्नाद्ध्येव खल्विमानि भूतानि जायन्ते। अन्नेन जातानि जीवन्ति। अन्नं प्रयन्त्यभिसंविशन्तीति। तद्विज्ञाय। पुनरेव वरुणं पितरमुपससार। अधीहि भगवो ब्रह्मेति। तꣳ होवाच। तपसा ब्रह्म विजिज्ञासस्व। तपो ब्रह्मेति। स तपोऽतप्यत। स तपस्तप्त्वा ॥१॥ इति द्वितीयोऽनुवाकः ॥

1. (He) realized food (i.e. Virāt, the gross Cosmic person) as Brahman. For it is verily from food that all these beings take birth, on food they subsist after being born, and they move towards and merege into food. Having realized that, he again approached his father Varuṇa with the (formal) request. 'O revered sir,

---

went on revolving in his mind what he had heard. That was his *tapaḥ*.

teach me Brahman.' To him he (Varuṇa) said: 'Crave to know Brahman well through concentration; concentration is Brahman.' He practised concentration. He, having practised concentration—.

Vyajānāt, he knew; *annam brahma iti*, food as Brahman; for food is endowed with the aforesaid characteristics. How? *Hi*, for; *annāt*, from food; *khalu eva*, indeed; *imāni bhūtāni jāyante*, these beings are born; *jātāni jīvanti*, having been born; they live *annena*, by food; and *prayanti abhisaṁviśanti*, they move towards and enter into; *annam*, food. Hence it is reasonable that food is Brahman. This is the idea. He having practised concentration in this way, and *tat vijñāya*, having known that food as Brahman, from its characteristics as well as reasoning; *varuṇam pitaram upasasāra*, approached his father Varuṇa; *punaḥ eva*, over again, being under doubt; with, *iti*, this (formal request); '*Adhīhi bhagavaḥ brahma*, O revered sir, teach me Brahman.'

Objection: What was, again, the occasion for his doubt?

The *answer* is: Because food is seen to have an origin.

Concentration is repeatedly inculcated in order to emphasise the fact of its being the best discipline. The idea is this: 'Concentration alone is your discipline till the description of Brahman can be pushed no further and till your desire to know becomes quietened. Through concentration alone, you crave to know Brahman.' The rest is easy.

CHAPTER III

प्राणो ब्रह्मेति व्यजानात्। प्राणाद्ध्येव खल्विमानि भूतानि जायन्ते। प्राणेन जातानि जीवन्ति। प्राणं प्रयन्त्यभिसंविशन्तीति। तद्विज्ञाय। पुनरेव वरुणं पितरमुपससार। अधीहि भगवो ब्रह्मेति। तꣳ होवाच। तपसा ब्रह्म विजिज्ञासस्व। तपो ब्रह्मेति। स तपोऽतप्यत। स तपस्तप्त्वा॥१॥ इति तृतीयोऽनुवाकः॥

1. (He) knew the vital force as Brahman;[1] for from the vital force, indeed, spring all these beings; having come into being, they live through the vital force; they move towards and enter into the vital force. Having known thus, he again approached his father Varuṇa with the (formal) request, 'O revered sir, teach me Brahman.' To him he (Varuṇa) said, 'Crave to know Brahman well through concentration; concentration is Brahman.' He practised concentration. He, having practised concentration—.

CHAPTER IV

मनो ब्रह्मेति व्यजानात्। मनसो ह्येव खल्विमानि भूतानि

[1] As Virāṭ (the food-Brahman) has an origin, Virāṭ could not fully answer the description. So Bhṛgu pushed on his inquiry to arrive at Hiraṇyagarbha, conceived of as possessing vital energy. Then he reached the same Hiraṇyagarbha as possessed of mental energy, and lastly as possessed of the energy of knowledge. (See footnotes, pp. 140–41.)

जायन्ते। मनसा जातानि जीवन्ति। मनः प्रयन्त्यभिसंविशन्तीति। तद्विज्ञाय। पुनरेव वरुणं पितरमुपससार। अधीहि भगवो ब्रह्मेति। तꣳ होवाच। तपसा ब्रह्म विजिज्ञासस्व। तपो ब्रह्मेति। स तपोऽतप्यत। स तपस्तप्त्वा ॥१॥ इति चतुर्थोऽनुवाकः ॥

1. (He) knew the mind as Brahman; for from the mind, indeed, spring all these beings; having been born, they are sustained by the mind; and they move towards and merge into the mind. Having known that, he approached his father Varuṇa again and made the (formal) request, 'O revered sir, teach me Brahman.' To him he (Varuṇa) said: 'Crave to know Brahman well through concentration; concentration is Brahman.' He practised concentration. He, having practised concentration—.

CHAPTER V

विज्ञानं ब्रह्मेति व्यजानात्। विज्ञानाद्ध्येव खल्विमानि भूतानि जायन्ते। विज्ञानेन जातानि जीवन्ति। विज्ञानं प्रयन्त्यभिसंविशन्तीति। तद्विज्ञाय। पुनरेव वरुणं पितरमुपससार। अधीहि भगवो ब्रह्मेति। तꣳ होवाच। तपसा ब्रह्म विजिज्ञासस्व। तपो ब्रह्मेति। स तपोऽतप्यत। स तपस्तप्त्वा ॥१॥ इति पञ्चमोऽनुवाकः ॥

1. (He) knew knowledge as Brahman; for from

knowledge, indeed, spring all these beings; having been born, they are sustained by knowledge; they move towards and merge in knowledge. Having known that, he approached his father Varuṇa again, with the (formal) request, 'O revered sir, teach me Brahman.' To him he (Varuṇa) said: 'Crave to know Brahman well through concentration; concentration is Brahman.' He practised concentration. He, having practised concentration—.

CHAPTER VI

आनन्दो ब्रह्मेति व्यजानात्। आनन्दाद्ध्येव खल्विमानि भूतानि जायन्ते। आनन्देन जातानि जीवन्ति। आनन्दं प्रयन्त्यभिसंविशन्तीति। सैषा भार्गवी वारुणी विद्या। परमे व्योमन्प्रतिष्ठिता। स य एवं वेद प्रतितिष्ठति। अन्नवानन्नादो भवति। महान्भवति प्रजया पशुभिर्ब्रह्मवर्चसेन। महान् कीर्त्या ॥१॥ इति षष्ठोऽनुवाकः ॥

1. (He) knew Bliss as Brahman; for from Bliss, indeed, all these beings originate; having been born, they are sustained by Bliss; they move towards and merge in Bliss. This knowledge realized by Bhṛgu and imparted by Varuṇa (starts from the food-self and) terminates in the supreme (Bliss), established in the cavity of the heart. He who knows thus becomes firmly established; he becomes the possessor of food and the eater of food; and he becomes great in progeny, cattle and the lustre of holiness, and great in glory.

Thus becoming pure in mind through concentration and failing to find the definition of Brahman, in its fullness, in the selves composed of the vital force etc., Bhṛgu penetrated inside by degrees, and with the help of concentration alone realized the innermost Bliss that is Brahman. Therefore, the idea conveyed by this topic is that anyone who is desirous of knowing Brahman should undertake concentration of the internal and external organs as the most excellent practice of *tapaḥ* (austerity).

Now, standing aside from the story, the Upaniṣad states the purport of the story in its own words: *sā eṣā*, this, then, is; the *vidyā*, knowledge; (which was) *bhārgavī*, realized by Bhṛgu; (and) *vāruṇī*, imparted by Varuṇa; (which) commencing from the self constituted by food, *pratiṣṭhitā*, culminates; in the supreme, non-dual Bliss that is lodged *parame vyoman*, in the cavity that is the supreme space within the heart. Anybody else, too, who realizes the Bliss that is Brahman by entering through this very process and through concentration alone as his aid—that man, too, in consequence of his knowledge culminating thus, gets established in the Bliss that is the supreme Brahman; that is to say, he becomes Brahman Itself.

Moreover, a visible result is being vouchsafed for him: *Annavān* has to be taken in the sense of one who is possessed of plenty of food, since knowledge would get no credit if the term meant simply possession of food as such, for that is a patent fact in the case of everybody. Similarly, *annādaḥ*, (derived in the sense of an eater of food), means that he is blest with good digestion. *Mahān bhavati*, he becomes great. In what does the greatness consist? The answer is: *prajayā*, in sons etc.; *paśubhiḥ*, in cows, horses, etc.; *brahmavarcasena*, in the lustre resulting from the control of external and internal organs, knowledge, etc. He becomes *mahān*, great; *kīrtyā*, through fame due to a virtuous life.

CHAPTER VII

अन्नं न निन्द्यात्। तद्व्रतम्। प्राणो वा अन्नम्। शरीर-मन्नादम्। प्राणे शरीरं प्रतिष्ठितम्। शरीरे प्राणः प्रतिष्ठितः। तदेतदन्नमन्ने प्रतिष्ठितम्। स य एतदन्नमन्ने प्रतिष्ठितं वेद प्रतितिष्ठति। अन्नवानन्नादो भवति। महान्भवति प्रजया पशुभिर्ब्रह्मवर्चसेन। महान् कीर्त्या ॥१॥ इति सप्तमोऽनु-वाकः ॥

1. His vow is that he should not deprecate food. The vital force is verily food, and the body is the eater of food. The body is fixed on the vital force. The vital force is lodged in the body. Thus (the body and vital force are both foods; and) one food is lodged in another. He who knows thus that one food is lodged in another, gets firmly established. He becomes a possessor and an eater of food. He becomes great in progeny, cattle, and the lustre of holiness, and great in glory.

Moreover, since Brahman is realized through the portal of food, *na nindyāt*, one should not deprecate; *annam*, food, just as one would not cavil at his teacher.

(This is) *tad-vratam*, a vow that is enjoined for him who knows Brahman thus. The inculcation of the vow is meant for the praise of food; and food is worthy of praise, since it is an aid to the realization of Brahman. *Prāṇaḥ vai annam*, the vital force is verily food, for the vital force is encased in the body. Anything that is encompassed by another becomes food of the latter; and *śarīre praṇaḥ pratiṣṭhitaḥ*, the vital force is lodged in the body; therefore the vital force is food, and *śarīram annādam*, the body is the eater. Similarly, the body, too, is food and the vital force is an eater. Why? Since *prāṇe śarīraṁ pratiṣṭhitam*, the body is fixed on the vital force, the continuation of the body being dependent on the later. Therefore both of these two—the body and the vital force—are (mutually) food and the eater. In the aspect of their being lodged in each other, they are food; and in the aspect of being the support of each other they are eaters. Hence both the vital force and the body are food and the eater. *Saḥ yaḥ*, he who; *veda*, knows; *etat annam anne pratiṣṭhitam*, this food as established on food; *pratitiṣṭhati*, becomes firmly established—in the very form of food and the eater. Moreover, he *bhavati*, becomes; *annavān*, a possessor of (plenty of) food; *annādaḥ*, an eater (i.e. a digester) of food. All these are to be explained as before.

CHAPTER VIII

अन्नं न परिचक्षीत। तद्व्रतम्। आपो वा अन्नम्। ज्योतिरन्नादम्। अप्सु ज्योतिः प्रतिष्ठितम्। ज्योतिष्याप:

प्रतिष्ठिताः। तदेतदन्नमन्ने प्रतिष्ठितम्। स य एतदन्नमन्ने प्रतिष्ठितं वेद प्रतितिष्ठति। अन्नवानन्नादो भवति। महा-न्भवति प्रजया पशुभिर्ब्रह्मवर्चसेन। महान्कीर्त्या॥१॥
इति अष्टमोऽनुवाकः॥

1. His vow is that he should not discard food. Water indeed is food; fire is the eater of food. Fire is established on water. Water resides in fire. Thus one food is lodged in another food. He who knows thus that one food is lodged in another, gets firmly established. He becomes a possessor and an eater of food. He becomes great in progeny, cattle, and the lustre of holiness, and great in glory.

Annam na paricakṣīta, he should not discard food. This is a vow for him, which is meant as a praise (of food) just as before. Thus the food, that is not ignored through ideas of good or bad, becomes eulogised and heightened in esteem. The idea, as explained before, should be similarly understood to be implied in the subsequent texts: *āpaḥ vai annam*, water indeed is food, etc.

CHAPTER IX

अन्नं बहु कुर्वीत। तद्व्रतम्। पृथिवी वा अन्नम्। आकाशोऽन्नादः। पृथिव्यामाकाशः प्रतिष्ठितः। आकाशे पृथिवी प्रतिष्ठिता। तदेतदन्नमन्ने प्रतिष्ठितम्। स य एत-

दन्नमन्ने प्रतिष्ठितं वेद प्रतितिष्ठति। अन्नवानन्नादो भवति। महान्भवति प्रजया पशुभिर्ब्रह्मवर्चसेन। महान् कीर्त्या ॥१॥
इति नवमोऽनुवाकः ॥

1. His vow is that he should make food plentiful. Earth is food; space is the eater of food. Space is placed in earth. Earth is placed in space. Thus one food is lodged in another food. He who knows thus that one food is lodged in another, gets firmly established. He becomes a possessor and an eater of food. He becomes great in progeny, cattle and the lustre of holiness, and great in glory.

The vow to make food plentiful is meant for one who worships fire and water as possessed of the attributes of food and the eater of food in the way that was mentioned by the text, 'fire resides in water,' etc. (in the preceding chapter).

CHAPTER X

न कंचन वसतौ प्रत्याचक्षीत। तद्व्रतम्। तस्माद्यया कया च विधया बह्वन्नं प्राप्नुयात्। अराध्यस्मा अन्नमित्याचक्षते। एतद्वै मुखतोऽन्नꣳ राद्धम्। मुखतोऽस्मा अन्नꣳ राध्यते। एतद्वै मध्यतोऽन्नꣳ राद्धम्। मध्यतोऽस्मा अन्नꣳ राध्यते। एतद्वा अन्ततोऽन्नꣳ राद्धम्। अन्ततोऽस्मा अन्नꣳ राध्यते ॥१॥ य एवं वेद। क्षेम इति वाचि। योगक्षेम इति प्राणापानयोः।

कर्मेति हस्तयोः। गतिरिति पादयोः। विमुक्तिरिति पायौ। इति मानुषीः समाज्ञाः। अथ दैवीः। तृप्तिरिति वृष्टौ। बलमिति विद्युति ॥२॥

1–2. His vow is that he should not refuse anyone come for shelter. Therefore one should collect plenty of food by whatsoever means he may. (And one should collect food for the further reason that) they say, 'Food is ready for him.' Because he offers cooked food in his early age with honour, food falls to his share in the early age with honour. Because he offers food in his middle age with medium courtesy, food falls to his share in his middle age with medium honour. Because he offers food in this old age with scant esteem, food falls to his share in old age with scant consideration. To him who knows thus (comes the result as described).

(Brahman is to be meditated on) as preservation in speech; as acquisition and preservation in exhaling and inhaling; as action in the hands; as movement in the feet; discharge in the anus. These are meditations on the human plane.

Then follow the divine ones. (Brahman is to be meditated on) as contentment in rain; as energy in lightning.

So also there is a vow for one who meditates on earth and space (as mutually the food and the eater): *na pratyācakṣīta*, he should not refuse; *kam cana*, anybody, whomsoever; *vasatau*, in the matter of dwelling. The meaning is that he should not turn back anybody who may come for shelter. Since, if shelter is given, food, too, must be supplied, therefore *yayā kayā ca vidhayā*, by any means whatsoever; *prāpnuyāt bahu annam*, he should get, i.e. collect, plenty of food. Since the enlightened people (i.e. meditators) possessed of food, *ācakśate*, say; '*Annam arādhi asmai*, food has been cooked for this man', and they do not refuse him by saying, 'There is no food', therefore also, one should acquire plenty of food. This is how this portion should be construed with the earlier. Moreover, the greatness of the gift of food is being stated: Food greets one back in that very manner and at that very period (of life) in which it is offered. How? That is being explained: *Etat vai*, the fact that; *annam*, food; *rāddham*, cooked; *mukhataḥ*, in early age, or with the best attitude, with veneration—; 'he offers to the guest seeking food', this much is to be added to complete the sentence. What result will he get? The answer is: *Asmai* for this one—for the giver of food; *annam rādhyate*, food is cooked; *mukhataḥ*, in the early age, or in the best manner. The idea is that food falls to his share just as it was offered. Similarly, *madhyataḥ* means during the middle part of life, and with middling courtesy. Thus, too, *antataḥ* means in the old age, and with scant courtesy, i.e. with discourtesy. In that very manner *annam rādhyate asmai*, food is cooked for him, food accrues to him. *Yaḥ evam veda*, he who knows thus—knows the greatness of food and the result of that gift as stated—, to him befalls the aforesaid result (of that gift).

Now is being stated a process of meditation on Brahman: *Kṣemaḥ* means the preservation of what has been acquired; Brahman is to be meditated on as existing *vāci*, in speech, in the form of preservation.

Yogaḥ means the acquisition of what is not in possession. Though these acquisition and preservation occur so long as exhaling and inhaling function, still they are not brought about by the mere fact of living. What are they, then, due to? They are caused by Brahman. Therefore Brahman is to be meditated on as existing *prāṇāpānayoḥ*, in exhalation and inhalation, in the form of acquisition and preservation. Similarly, with regard to the other succeeding cases Brahman is to be meditated on as identified with those (respective) things. Since work is done by Brahman, Brahman is to be meditated on as existing *hastayoḥ*, in the hands; *karma iti*, in the form of work; *gatiḥ iti*, as movement; *pādayoḥ*, in the feet: *vimuktiḥ iti*, as discharge; *pāyau*, in the anus. *Iti*, these are: *samājñāḥ*, cognitions, perceptions, i.e. meditations; which are *mānuṣīḥ* (should be rather *mānuṣyaḥ*), pertaining to men, belonging to the physical body. *Atha*, after this; *daivīḥ*, (should be rather *daivyaḥ*), the divine, the meditations pertaining to the gods—are being related. *Tṛptiḥ iti vṛṣṭau*, as satisfaction in rain. Since rain causes contentment by producing food etc., Brahman is to be meditated on as existing in rain in the form of contentment. Similarly, in the case of other things, Brahman is to be meditated on as existing in those forms. So also It is to be meditated on as energy in lightning.

यश इति पशुषु। ज्योतिरिति नक्षत्रेषु। प्रजातिरमृतमानन्द इत्युपस्थे। सर्वमित्याकाशे। तत्प्रतिष्ठेत्युपासीत। प्रतिष्ठावान् भवति। तन्मह इत्युपासीत। महान्भवति।

तन्मन इत्युपासीत। मानवान्भवति ॥३॥ तन्नम इत्युपासीत। नम्यन्तेऽस्मै कामाः। तद्ब्रह्मेत्युपासीत। ब्रह्मवान्भवति। तद्ब्रह्मणः परिमर इत्युपासीत। पर्येणं म्रियन्ते द्विषन्तः सपत्नाः। परि येऽप्रिया भ्रातृव्याः। स यश्चायं पुरुषे। यश्चासावादित्ये। स एकः ॥४॥

3–4. Brahman is to be worshipped as fame in beasts; as light in the stars; as procreation, immortality, and joy in the generative organ; as everything in space. One should meditate on that Brahman as the support; thereby one becomes supported. One should meditate on that Brahman as great; thereby one becomes great. One should meditate on It as thinking; thereby one becomes able to think. One should meditate on It as bowing down; thereby the enjoyable things bow down to one. One should meditate on It as the most exalted; thereby one becomes exalted. One should meditate on It as Brahman's medium of destruction; thereby the adversaries that envy such a one die, and so do the enemies whom this one dislikes.

He that is here in the human person, and He that is there in the sun, are one.

(Brahman is to be worshipped) as *yaśaḥ*, fame; *paśuṣu*, among animals;[1] as *jyotiḥ*, light, *nakṣatreṣu*, in the stars. *Prajātiḥ*, procreation; *amṛtam*, immortality, getting of immortality — this being brought about by

[1] I.e. as existing in cattle-wealth, since wealth makes a man famous.

the son's repaying the debts; *ānandaḥ*, happiness—all these originate from the organ of generation, and Brahman is to be meditated on as existing in those forms in the generative organ. Since *sarvam*, everything; is placed *ākāśe*, in space (or the Unmanifested), therefore one should meditate thus: 'All that is in space is Brahman.' And that space, too, is Brahman. Therefore that (space-Brahman) is to be meditated on as the support of all. By meditating on the attribute of 'being the sustainer', one becomes well established. So also with regard to the previous cases, it is to be understood that any effect that is produced by any of the factors,[1] is but Brahman only; and by meditating on that (effect as Brahman) one becomes possessed of it. This also follows from another Vedic text, 'As he worships Him, so he becomes' (Mud. III.3). *Upāsīta*, one should worship; *tat*, that (Brahman), *mahaḥ iti*, as possessed of greatness; (thereby) *bhavati mahān*, one becomes great. (Brahman should be meditated on as) *manaḥ*, thinking; (thereby) *bhavati mānavān*, he becomes able to think. *Tat namaḥ*, etc.: *namaḥ* means bowing down, (possessed of suppleness); Brahman is to be worshipped as possessed of suppleness; (thereby) *kāmāḥ*, desires, things that are desired, i.e. enjoyable things; *namyante*, bow down; *asmai*, to such a meditator. One should meditate on *tat*, that Brahman; *brahman iti*, as the most exalted; (thereby) one *bhavati brahmavān*, becomes possessed of that quality of being the most exalted.[2] *Tat brahmaṇaḥ* etc.: *parimaraḥ* is derived in the sense of

[1] E.g. preservation, produced by speech, is Brahman.
[2] Like Virāt, possessed of all gross means of enjoyment.

that in which die, from all sides, the five gods, viz Lightning, Rain, Moon, Sun, and Fire. Therefore air is their *parimaraḥ*, destruction—in accordance with another Vedic text, ('Air [Virāt] is, indeed, the place of merger'), (Ch. IV.iii. 1). Again, this very air is non-different from space; hence space is *brahmaṇaḥ parimaraḥ*, Brahman's medium of destruction. *Upāsīta*, one should meditate on; *tat*, that space, which is non-different from air,[1] as Brahman's medium of destruction. (As a result) *sapatnāḥ*, adversaries; who are *dviṣataḥ*, envious; *enam*, towards this man; *pari mriyante*, part with their lives. There may be adversaries who are not envious; hence the singling out in this form, 'the envious adversaries'. Those adversaries that are envious towards this man (die). Moreover, *ye bhrātṛvyāḥ*, those adversaries of this man; who are *apriyāḥ*, disliked (by him), though they may not be spiteful—they, too, die.

Beginning with the text, 'the vital force is, indeed, food, and the body is the eater of food', and ending with space, creation has been shown as food and the eater of food.

Objection: It might have been said so; what of that?

Answer: Thereby is proved this: Worldly existence, comprising enjoyment and enjoyership, pertain only to created things, but not to the Self; yet it is superimposed on the Self through ignorance.

Objection: The Self, too, is a product of the supreme Self, and hence the Self's worldly existence is quite in order.

[1] Since air comes out of space.

Answer: No, for the Upaniṣad refers to the entry of the Transcendental (Brahman). In the text, 'Having created that, He entered into that very thing' (II.vi.1), the entry into creation is predicated verily of the transcendental supreme Self which is, indeed, the cause of space etc. Hence the Self which has entered into creation as the individual soul is none other than the supermundane, supreme Self. Moreover, this follows from the propriety of the same entity being the subject of the two verbs in the expression, 'having created, he entered'. If the two verbs implying creation and entry have the same subject, then only is the suffix *ktvā* (-ing) justifiable.

Objection: But the one which enters undergoes a change.

Answer: No, since entry has been explained away by giving it a different meaning (II.vi.).

Objection: May not the entry be through a change of attributes, since there is such a categorical text, 'entering in the form of this individual soul . . .' (Ch. VI.iii.2)?

Answer: No, since reinstatement into the earlier mode is spoken of in 'Thou art That' (Ch. VI. viii-xvi).

Objection: It is a meditation, involving the superimposition of the greater on the less, which is calculated to remove a change that has come over one (of the two).

Answer: No, for the two are placed on the same pedestal in the text, 'That is truth, That is the Self; and thou art That' (*ibid*).

Objection: The worldly state of the individual soul is a perceived reality.

Answer: No, for the perceiver cannot be perceived (Bṛ.II.iv.14).

Objection: The (individual) Self, as endowed with worldly attributes, is perceived.

Answer: Not so; (for if they are real attributes of the Self, then), since the attributes of a thing are non-separable from the substratum, they cannot reasonably become objects of perception, just as heat and light (of fire) cannot be subjected to burning or illumination (by fire).

Objection: The soul is inferred to be possessed of sorrow etc., since fear etc. are seen (in it).

Answer: No, for fear etc. and sorrow cannot be the qualities of the perceiver (soul), since they are perceived (by it).

Objection: This runs counter to the (Sāṁkhya) scripture promulgated by Kapila, and to the science of logic built up by Kaṇāda and others.

Answer: Not so; for if they have no (logical) basis or if they are opposed to the Vedas, it is reasonable to call them erroneous. And from the Vedas as well as from reasoning, the Self is proved to be transcendental. Besides, this follows from the unity of the Self.

Objection: How is that unity?

Answer: That is being stated (in *saḥ yaḥ ca ayam* etc.). The whole of the text, *saḥ yaḥ ca ayam* etc., is to be construed as already explained (II.viii.5).

स य एवंवित्। अस्माल्लोकात्प्रेत्य। एतमन्नमयमात्मानमुपसंक्रम्य। एतं प्राणमयमात्मानमुपसंक्रम्य। एतं मनोमयमात्मानमुपसंक्रम्य। एतं विज्ञानमयमात्मानमुपसंक्रम्य।

एतमानन्दमयमात्मानमुपसंक्रम्य । इमाँल्लोकान्कामान्नी काम-
रूप्यनुसंचरन् । एतत् साम गायन्नास्ते । हा३वु हा३वु
हा३वु ॥५॥ अहमन्नमहमन्नमहमन्नम् । अहमन्नादो३ऽहमन्ना-
दो३ऽहमन्नादः । अहꣳ श्लोककृदहꣳ श्लोककृदहꣳ श्लोककृत् ।
अहमस्मि प्रथमजा ऋता३स्य । पूर्वं देवेभ्योऽमृतस्य ना३भायि ।
यो मा ददाति स इदेव मा३ऽऽवाः । अहमन्नमन्नमदन्त-
मा३द्मि । अहं विश्वं भुवनमभ्यभवा३म् । सुवर्न ज्योतीः ।
य एवं वेद । इत्युपनिषत् ॥६॥ इति दशमोऽनुवाकः ॥

इति भृगुवल्ली समाप्ता ॥

5–6. He who knows thus, attains, after desisting from this world, this self made of food. After attaining this self made of food, then, attaining this self made of vital force, then attaining this self made of mind, then attaining this self made of intelligence, then attaining this self made of bliss, and roaming over these worlds with command over food at will and command over all forms at will, he continues singing this *sāma* song: 'Oho! Oho! Oho! I am the food, I am the food, I am the food; I am the eater, I am the eater, I am the eater; I am the unifier, I am the unifier, I am the unifier; I am (Hiraṇyagarbha) the first born of this world consisting of the formed and the formless, I (as Virāṭ) am earlier than the gods. I am the navel of immortality. He who offers me thus (as food), protects me just as I am. I, food as I am, eat him up who eats food without offering. I defeat (i.e. engulf) the entire universe. Our effulgence is like that of the sun. He who knows thus (gets such results). This is the Upaniṣad.

Starting from the self constituted by food, and by degrees *ānandamayam ātmānam upasaṁkramya*, reaching the self, constituted by joy;[1] *āste*, he sits (continues); *gāyan*, singing on; *etat sāma*, this *sāma* (song).

The meaning of the *Ṛg-mantra*—'*Satyam jñānam* etc.—Brahman is truth, knowledge,' etc. (II.i.)—has been explained elaborately in the Part *On Bliss*, which is an exposition of it. But the meaning of the statement of its result contained in the text, 'He enjoys, as identified with the all-knowing Brahman, all desirable things simultaneously' (II.i.), has not been elaborated. Now the following text begins, since it remains to be shown what these results are, what the objects of all those desires are, and how he enjoys them simultaneously in his identity with Brahman. As to that, in the story of the father and the son (in Part III), which is supplementary to the knowledge imparted earlier (in Part II), concentration has been spoken of as a means for the knowledge of Brahman. Besides, it has been shown how creation, counting from the vital force and ending with space, can be divided into the eater and the eaten; and the meditations on Brahman have been referred to. Furthermore, all the enjoyments that there are and pertain to diverse products like space etc., have been shown to be the results of multifarious means that are systematically related to their results. On the attainment of unity, however, there cannot logically remain any desire or desirer, since all diversity becomes

[1] II.viii.5 refers to liberation after death, whereas this portion of the present text refers to liberation even while living (*jīvanmukti*). —Ś.

merged in the Self. So how can such a knower enjoy all desires simultaneously in the state of identity with Brahman? In answer to this question it is being said that this is possible because of his becoming the Self of all. To the question, 'How is there an attainment of identity with the Self of all?'—the answer is: As a result of the knowledge of the identity of the Self existing in the individual and the sun, having discarded excellence and non-excellence, having attained in succession the selves—starting with the one made of food and ending with the one constituted by bliss—which are fancied through ignorance, and having realized, as a result, Brahman which is truth, knowledge, and infinity, which is unperceivable etc. by nature, which is natural Bliss, and which is birthless, immortal, fearless, and non-dual; and then (that man of knowledge) *anusaṁcaran*, wandering; on *imān lokān*, these worlds—the earth etc.; this is how the expression *imān lokān* is to be construed with the remote word *anusaṁcaran*. Wandering how? (Becoming) *kāmānnī*—one who gets *anna*, food, according to *kāma*, wish, is *kāmānnī*, (having command over food at will); similarly, (becoming *kāmarūpī*) one who gets *rūpas*, forms, according to his wish is *kāmarūpī*; wandering on all these worlds, in his identity with all, i.e. perceiving all these worlds as the Self. 'What does he do? *Etat sāma gāyan āste*: *āste*, he continues; *gāyan*, singing, uttering; *etat sāma*, this *sāma* (song). Brahman Itself is the *sāma*, because It is *sama*, equal, non-different from everything. (So the idea is): He continues declaring the unity of the Self as also announcing, for the good of others, the result of that knowledge consisting in absolute contentment.

How does he sing? (He sings): *Hā-ā-ā-vu, hā-ā-ā-vu, hā-ā-ā- vu*; the expression is used in the sense of 'oho' to indicate supreme surprise. What, again, is that surprise? The answer is: Although I am really the untainted, nondual Self, still I am *annam*, food; as also *annādaḥ*, the eater of food. Moreover, *aham*, I myself; am the *ślokakṛt*: *śloka* means union — union of food and the eater of food; the conscious being encompassing that union is the *ślokakṛt*. Or the expression may mean this: I bring about the assemblage of food itself, which is naturally meant for somebody other than itself, viz the eater, and which becomes diversified owing to this very fact. The three repetitions are meant for expressing astonishment. *Aham asmi*, I am; *prathamajāḥ* (i.e. *prathamajaḥ*), the first born (Hiraṇyagarbha); *ṛtasya*, of this world, consisting of the formed and the formless; and (I am Virāṭ which is) *pūrvam*, earlier; *devebhyaḥ*, than the gods. (I am) *nābhiḥ* (*nābhāyī*) the navel, centre; *amṛtasya*, of immortality, i.e. the immortality of living beings is in my keeping. *Yaḥ*, anyone who; *dadāti mā*, offers me as food, to those who beg food — talks of me as the food; *saḥ*, he; *iti*, in this way; *āvāḥ*, i.e. *avati*, protects (me); *evam*, intact and just as I am. On the contrary, *aham*, I; who am but *annam*, the food, for the present; *admi*, eat up; *adantam annam*, that eater of food — any other man, who eats food without offering me in the form of food — at the proper time — to those who ask.

At this point someone may say: 'If this be so, I am

afraid of liberation that consists in becoming the Self of all. Let my worldly existence itself continue; for even though liberated, I shall still be food to be eaten by somebody.' (The answer is:) Do not entertain such a fear, for the enjoyment of all the desirable things falls within the range of relative existence. But this man of knowledge has become Brahman by transcending, through illumination, all that is described as the eater and the eaten which fall within the domain of empirical experience and which are the creations of ignorance. For him there exists no separate thing of which he can be afraid. Hence there is nothing to be afraid of in liberation.

Objection: If this be so, then what is meant by saying, 'I am the eaten and the eater'?

Answer: This phenomenal existence, constituted by the eater and the eaten, which endures as a product, is nothing but a phenomenon; it is not a real substance. But though it is so, still, having in view the fact that it exists because of Brahman and that it is reduced to a nonentity apart from Brahman, this phenomenon is referred to in the text, 'I am food,' etc., for the sake of recommending the state of identity with Brahman which follows from the knowledge of Brahman. Therefore, when ignorance is eradicated, there cannot exist for the man identified with Brahman any remnant of such taints as fear which are the creations of ignorance. Accordingly, *aham*, I; *abhyabhavām*, overwhelm, engulf in my supreme nature as God; *viśvam*, the whole; *bhuvanam*, universe—derivatively meaning that which is enjoyed by all beings counting from Brahmā, or that on which all creatures are born. *Suvaḥ na joytiḥ*: *Suvaḥ* is the sun; *na* expresses similitude. The meaning is: Our *jyotiḥ*, effulgence; is ever-shining *suvaḥ na* like the sun. *Iti upaniṣad*, this is the knowledge of the supreme Self, inculcated in the two Parts (II and III). To him come the aforesaid fruits who, like Bhṛgu, masters the above mentioned Upaniṣad through practice of great concentration after the acquisition of control over the inner and outer organs, dispassionateness, imperturbability, and concentration.

ॐ सह नाववतु। सह नौ भुनक्तु। सह वीर्यं करवावहै।
तेजस्वि नावधीतमस्तु मा विद्विषावहै।

ॐ शान्तिः शान्तिः शान्तिः।

INDEX TO THE SECTIONS

अग्निः पूर्वरूपम्	I.iii.2
अथातः संहिताया उपनिषदं	I.iii.1
अथाधिज्यौतिषम्	I.iii.2
अथाधिप्रजम्	I.iii.3
अथाधिविद्यम्	I.iii.2
अथाध्यात्मम्	I.iii.5,
,,	I.vii.1
अधरा हनुः पूर्वरूपम्	I.iii.4
अन्नं न परिचक्षीत	III.viii.1
अन्नं न निन्द्यात्	III.vii.1
अन्नं बहु कुर्वीत	III.ix.1
अन्नं ब्रह्मेति व्यजानात्	III.ii.1
अन्नं हि भूतानां ज्येष्ठम्	II.ii.1
अन्नाद्वै प्रजाः प्रजायन्ते	II.ii.1
अन्नाद् भूतानि जायन्ते	II.ii.1
असद्वा इदमग्र आसीत्	II.vii.1
असन्नेव स भवति	II.vi.1
अहमन्नमहमन्नम्	III.x.6
अहमस्मि प्रथमजा	III.x.6
अहं वृक्षस्य रेरिवा	I.x.1
आकाशशरीरं ब्रह्म	I.vi.2
आचार्य पूर्वरूपम्	I.iii.2
आनन्दो ब्रह्मेति व्यजानात्	III.vi.1
आनन्दाद्ध्येव खल्विमानि	III.vi.1
आप्नोति स्वाराज्यम्	I.vi.2
आमायन्तु ब्रह्मचारिणः	I.iv.2
आवहन्ती वितन्वाना	I.iv.1
एतमानन्दमयमात्मानम्	II.viii.5,
,,	III.x.5
एतं ह वाव न तपति	II.ix.1
एष आदेशः एष उपदेशः	I.xi.4
ओमिति ब्रह्म	I.viii.1
को ह्येवान्यात् कः प्राण्यात्	II.vii.1
क्षेम इति वाचि	III.x.2
तत्सृष्ट्वा तदेवानुप्राविशत्	II.vi.1
तदनुप्रविश्य सच्च त्यच्चाभवत्	I.iii.3 / II.vi.1
तन्नम इत्युपासीत	III.x.4
तपसा ब्रह्म विजिज्ञासस्व	III.ii.1
तस्माद्वा एतस्मादन्नरसमयात्	II.ii.1
तस्माद्वा एतस्मादात्मन	II.i.1
तस्यैष एव शारीर आत्मा	II.iii.1
देवपितृकार्याभ्यां	I.xi.2
न कंचन वसतौ प्रत्याचक्षीत	III.x.1
नो इतराणि	I.xi.3
पाङ्क्तं बा इदं सर्वम्	I.vii.1
पृथिवी पूर्वरूपम्	I.iii.1
पृथिव्यन्तरिक्षं द्यौर्दिशः	I.vii.1
प्राणं देवा अनु प्राणन्ति	II.iii.1
प्राणो व्यानोऽपान	I.vii.1
प्राणो ब्रह्मेति व्यजानात्	III.iii.1
ब्रह्मविदाप्नोति परम्	II.i.1

भीषाऽस्माद्वातः पवते	II.viii.1	रसो वै सः	II.vii.1
भूरित्यग्नौ प्रतितिष्ठति	I.vi.1	विज्ञानं ब्रह्मेति	III.v.1
भूर्भुवः सुवरिति	I.v.1	विज्ञानं यज्ञं तनुते	II.v.1
भृगुर्वै वारुणिः	III.i.1	वेदमनूच्याचार्योऽन्तेवासिनम्	I.xi.1
मनो ब्रह्मेति व्यजानात्	III.iv.1	शं नो मित्रः शं वरुणः	I.i.1,
मह इति, तद्ब्रह्म	I.v.1	,,	I.xii.1
मह इति ब्रह्म	I.v.3	श्रोत्रियस्य चाकामहतस्य	II.viii.1
मह इत्यादित्यः	I.v.2	स एको मनुष्यगन्धर्वाणाम्	II.viii.2
माता पूर्वरूपम्	I.iii.3	सत्यं ज्ञानमनन्तं ब्रह्म	II.i.1
यतो वा इमानि भूतानि	III.i.1	सत्यं वद धर्मं चर	I.xi.1
यतो वाचो निवर्तन्ते	II.iv.1,	स य एवंवित्	III.x.5
,,	II.ix.1	स य एषोऽन्तर्हृदय	I.vi.1
यदा ह्येवैष एतस्मिन्	II.vii.1	स यश्चायं पुरुषे	II.viii.5
यद्वै तत् सुकृतं	II.vii.1	सह नाववतु सह नौ भुनक्तु	II.i.
यश इति पशुषु	III.x.3	सह नौ यशः	I.iii.1
यशो जनेऽसानि	I.iv.3	सुवरित्यादित्ये	I.vi.2
यश्छन्दसामृषभो	I.iv.1	सैषाऽऽनन्दस्य मीमांसा	II.viii.1
ये तत्र ब्राह्मणाः संमर्शिनः	I.xi.4	सोऽकामयत	II.vi.1
ये के चास्मच्छ्रेयांसो	I.xi.3		